# This Book Is The Property of:

Student's Name _____

School's Name _____

County_____

City _____

Student's Address _____

Phone # _____ E-Mail _____

Month _____ Date _____ Year _____

**Special Note:**

Pupils whom purchased this textbook should feel free to write on any page or mark any part of it in any way he or she sees fit. This textbook must be used as an instructional text and a workbook by the pupils.

Teachers should see that the pupil's name and basic information are clearly written in ink in the spaces above.

**This textbook is not for resale. No part of this textbook should be photocopied or reproduced. Violators will be prosecuted under international copyright laws, and a restitution fine of $500,000.00 USD will be brought against anyone or institution found in violation.**

# Grade 1 Language Arts for Liberian Schools Fundamentals, First Edition

## Emmanuel Clarke

**President/CEO**
E. Sumo Clarke
Author and Professor

**Vice President**
Miatta Stella Herring
School Publishing & Sr. Marketing Negotiator

**VP for Administration**
Michael Dundas
**Visual Artist**
Laura Cuevas

**Sales and Marketing Rep.**
Princess G. Dennis

**Senior Production Editor**
Bethany Storrings
**Graphic Artist**
Oudvin Cassell

**Market Rep.**
Jonathan Reeves

COPYRIGHT© 2015 Clarke Publishing and Consulting Group, Inc. Clarke Publishing™ is a trademark used herein under license.

Printed in the United States of America and the Republic of Liberia, West Africa

1 2 3 4 5 6 7 8 9 **CP** 09 08 07 06 05

For more information, contact Clarke Publishing and Consulting Group, Inc., 54 Meredith Road, Hamilton, NJ 08610.
Or find us on the World Wide Web at: www.clarkepublish.com to place an order or get technical support for your product.

ALL RIGHTS RESERVED. No part of this work covered by the copyright hereon may be reproduced or used in any form or by any means—graphic, electronic, or mechanical, including photocopying, recording, taping, Web distribution, or information storage and retrieval systems—without the written permission of the publisher.

For permission to use material from this text or any of our products, contact us by

Tel (609) 581-9770 USA or
    +231-886103907 (Liberia)
www.clarkepublish.com
To Place an Order:
Tel (609) 581-9770 USA or
    Online Only

DISCLAIMER
Clarke Publishing and Consulting Group, Inc. reserves the right to revise this publication and make changes from time to time in its content without notice.
ISBN 978-0-9898042-5-7
Copyright © 2015 by Clarke Publishing and Consulting Group, Inc.
All rights reserved. This book or any portion thereof may not be reproduced or used in any manner whatsoever without the expressed written permission of the publisher except

for the use of brief quotations in a book review. Violators are subject to criminal lawsuit and a US $500,000.00 fine.

# PREFACE

*Golden Minds Grade 1 Language Arts For Liberian Schools Fundamentals—First Edition,* introduces English grammar and mechanics in an easy-to-learn format to the Liberian first graders. This short, yet intensive, text-workbook provides practical, varied, and meaningful new content and exercises that will stimulate students' interests.

**Proven Instructional Design**
This 1st edition of Golden Minds Grade 1 Language Arts for Liberian Schools: Fundamentals—First Edition uses an easy to follow self-teaching, highly motivational, classroom-tested plan of instruction that will meet a variety of needs and expectations. This one-of-a-kind, user-friendly approach has proven effective for a wide range of students, both in the United States, Singapore, and in many East African nations. This textbook can be used as a text for basic English, basic Language Arts, or Developmental English, or as a supplemental text for other foundational English classes.

**Key Features That Ensure Success**
This popular text-workbook covers the basics of Alphabet in pictures, the Eight Parts of Speech, grammar, punctuation, capitalization, numbers in words, word choices, spelling, vocabulary, subject verb agreement, reading comprehension, writing and more.

**Objectives.** Each chapter begins with objectives for students' mastery upon completion of the chapter.

**Well-Organized Format.** Subject matter is organized into small, easily mastered segments. Each segment is color coded to covers a specific part of the chapter.

**Extensive Examples.** Examples and analyses explain and clarify the concepts and rules presented. End of chapter review and test help define concepts and reinforce learning.

**Exercises.** These exercises, which occur throughout the chapters, allow students to check their understanding of the concepts presented. This is the Clarke Publishing English Learning Series approach to educating the Liberian students.

**Applications.** End of Chapter applications and evaluations provide extensive hands-on practice to further reinforce understanding of concepts presented in a chapter. Varied content and difficulty in these sentences and paragraphs will challenge and stimulate a wide range of abilities and interests. A Writing Activity in Chapter 6 gives students the opportunity to reinforce and strengthen their writing skills. Each chapter includes at least one or more review that emphasizes topics from throughout the chapter and a Comprehensive Review and Practice Test that adds topics from previous chapters.

**Posttest.** The Posttests show students how well they understood and can apply what they have learned from a chapter.

**Color Coded Headers.** The color coded chapter headers let students know where in the chapter they are. The headers are organized as follow: Lime Green Header reviews letters of the alphabet, color, and number and sequence. The Aqua Blue Header focuses on key concepts within the chapter. The India Green Header is used for mid chapter reviews and hands-on practice within the chapter. The Blue Green Header evaluates students' understanding of key concepts from the chapter. The Dark Pink Header is for hands-on activities. The focus is to let students practice what was learned in the chapter.

**Website.** Additional materials can be found on the publisher's website. The Grade 1 Language Arts For Liberian Schools: Fundamentals—First Edition, publisher's website offers chapter review quizzes, Proofreading Challenge activities, flashcards, a glossary, links to useful sites, and other helpful materials.

## Acknowledgements

The Clarke Publishing and Consulting Group, CP&CG English Learning Series would not be the leading Language Arts education series without the contributions of outstanding publishing professionals. As always, we would like to thank all those who spent hundreds of hours in helping us bring this book to a successful completion. I would like to thank the staff at Clarke Publishing and Consulting Group for their invaluable service to this one of a kind organization.

## About The Author

**Emmanuel Clarke**

Holds a B.S. in Engineering, and Masters (MSIS) in Information System, and Project Management (MSPM) from the New Jersey Institute of Technology, NJIT. He has a certificates in Instructional Design and Development from Langevin Learning Service, and is an Oracle Certified Professional, OCP. He is currently a Ph.D candidate in Human Centered Computing at the New Jersey Institute of Technology.

Emmanuel has more than 10 years of teaching experience at the university level. He is the author of several books. He lives and work in both North Carolina and the Republic of Liberia with his wife and four children. He enjoys farming cooking, running, bungee jumping, hiking, meeting new and interesting people, writing, reading and making fun.

# TABLE OF CONTENTS

Preface ............................................................. i
Acknowledgments ....................................... ii
About The Author ...................................... ii

**Chapter 1** ..................................................... 1
Introduction ................................................... 2
The 26 Letters of the Alphabet ................ 3
Putting All Together .................................... 7
How Words Are Created ............................ 8
Putting It All Together ............................... 13
Putting It All Together ............................... 18
How Words Are Created ........................... 19
Putting All Together .................................. 23
Let's Find Out ............................................. 24

**Chapter 2** ................................................... 30
Courtesy ...................................................... 31
Respect ........................................................ 30
The Golden Rules ...................................... 31
Greetings ..................................................... 32
Naming Words ........................................... 34
The Eight Parts of Speech ...................... 37
A Poem About Singular Nouns .............. 39
Putting It All Together ............................... 40
Let's Find Out ............................................. 41

**Chapter 3** ................................................... 46
The Eight Parts of Speech ...................... 46
Rules for Plural Nouns ............................. 47
Putting It All Together ............................... 52
The Types of Sentences .......................... 57
End Marks ................................................... 60
Reading and Poetry .................................. 61
The Man And The King ............................ 62
The Story of Nuumba ............................... 63
Let's Find Out ............................................. 67

**Chapter 4** ................................................... 72
Adjectives .................................................... 72

Putting It All Together ............................... 80
Numbers Into Words ................................ 81
Rhymes ........................................................ 89
Putting It All Together ............................... 91
Poem And Story Time ............................... 93
Liberians Do Not Answer Questions ..... 93
Our Journey To Monrovia ........................ 96
L.I.B .............................................................. 97
Let's Find Out ............................................. 98

**Chapter 5** ................................................. 102
Phonics ...................................................... 102
Action Verbs ............................................. 106
Fatu And The Tricky Blind Man .......... 107
Putting It All Together ............................. 111
Adjectives and Articles .......................... 112
Contractions ............................................. 116
A Poem About Contractions ................. 116
Putting It All Together ............................. 119
Negative Sentences ................................ 120
Compound Words .................................... 122
Fine Time ................................................... 124
Putting It All Together ............................. 125
Let's Find Out ........................................... 126

**Chapter 6** ................................................. 130
Review of English .................................... 130
Review of the Alphabet .......................... 134
Review of Singular Nouns ..................... 136
Review of Rhymes ................................... 138
Story and Dramatization ........................ 140
How Liberia Was Founded .................... 140
Review of The Days and Year .............. 142
Putting It All Together ............................. 143
Fun With Poetry ....................................... 144
Writing Activities ...................................... 145
Glossary .................................................... 160
Index ........................................................... 164
Photo Credits ........................................... 167

# CHAPTER ONE OBJECTIVES

The Alphabet .................. 3
Farmer .......................... 3
Africa ............................ 3
pet ................................. 4
nail ............................. 12
orange ....................... 12
peanut ....................... 15

Nefertiti ..................... 15
star ............................ 16
turtle ......................... 17
umbrella ................... 17
van ............................ 20
X-ray ......................... 21
zoo ............................ 22

# Introduction

## INTRODUCTION: GETTING TO KNOW ONE ANOTHER

**Everybody has a name.**

Everything has a name.

Some people have the same names.

**We use names to identify things, people, and places.**

My name is Sunday.

I am in the 1<sup>st</sup> Grade.

Sunday is a male.
Sunday is a boy.
Sunday is also the first day of the week.

FIGURE 1-1 Sunday in his classroom reading to his classmates

My name is Mary.

I have a puppy.

Mary is a female.
Mary is also a girl.

FIGURE 1-2 Mary and her puppy in the background

# Chapter 1

## THE 26 LETTERS OF THE ALPHABET: HOW THEY FORM WORDS

**A** is the first (1ˢᵗ) letter of the alphabet.

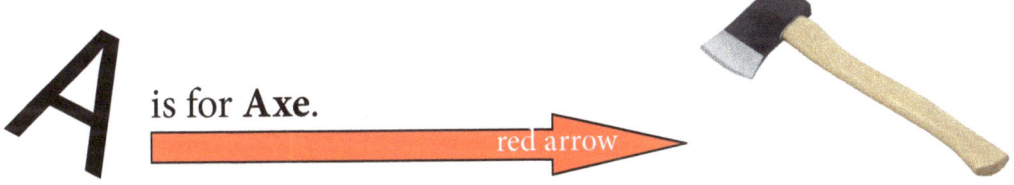

A is for **Axe**.

FIGURE 1-3 A farmer uses an axe for farming

A farmer uses an axe to cut down big trees.

**A farmer is a person who makes a farm or a garden.**

Can you think about other things an axe is used for?

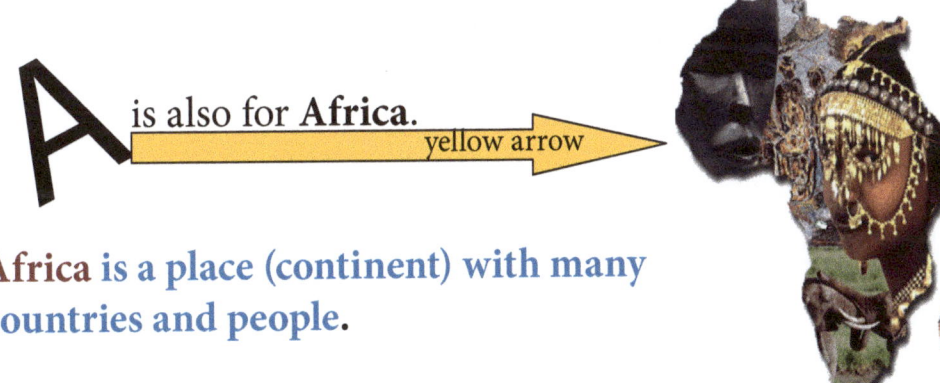

A is also for **Africa**.

**Africa is a place (continent) with many countries and people.**

FIGURE 1-4 The map of Africa. Liberia is a country in Africa where you live

# The Alphabet

## THE 26 LETTERS OF THE ALPHABET: HOW THEY FORM WORDS

B is the second (2nd) letter of the alphabet.

B is for **Boy**. → blue arrow

Sunday is a boy.

A male child is also called a **boy**.

Most boys have short hair.

FIGURE 1-5 Shows Sunday and Mary reading in class

C is the third (3rd) letter of the alphabet.

C is for **Cat**. → green arrow

A **cat** is a pet.

A **pet** is any animal we keep in our homes.

FIGURE 1-6 A picture of a white cat. Cat is a house pet that can be found in Liberia

# Chapter 1

## THE 26 LETTERS OF THE ALPHABET: HOW THEY FORM WORDS

**D** is the fourth (4th) letter of the alphabet.

**D** is for **Dog**. →orange arrow→

A dog is a pet.

**Pet** is any animal we keep in our homes.

A dog is also called human's best friend.

FIGURE 1-7 A picture of a dog wearing a "Made in Liberia" T-shirt

**E** is the fifth (5th) letter of the alphabet.

**E** is for **Egg**. →violet arrow→

An egg comes from a hen.

Egg is a food we fry or boil to eat.

What other things do people do with eggs?

FIGURE 1-8 A picture of a white egg. Eggs come from a female chicken called hen

# The Alphabet

## THE 26 LETTERS OF THE ALPHABET: HOW THEY FORM WORDS

**F** is the sixth (6<sup>th</sup>) letter of the Alphabet.

**F** is for Fish. →gray arrow→

FIGURE 1-9 A picture of a fish

Fish live in water.

We eat fish for food.

**G** is the seventh (7<sup>th</sup>) letter of the Alphabet.

**G** is for Goat. →pink arrow→

Goats live on a farm.

FIGURE 1-10 A picture of a male goat. A male goat is called, billy goat. A billy goat smells very bad.

Goats eat grass for food.

What are the names of other animals that eat grass for food?

Do people eat grass for food like goats and other animals do?

Why or why not?

# Chapter 1

**WHAT HAVE WE LEARNED SO FAR? PUTTING IT ALL TOGETHER**

### Vocabulary

1. Axe ▶
2. Boy ▶
3. Cat ▶
4. Dog ▶
5. Egg ▶
6. Fish ▶
7. Goat ▶

### Sequences and Numbers

**First** (1ˢᵗ) Means **1** .................... **Second** (2ⁿᵈ) Means **2**

**Third** (3ʳᵈ) Means **3** .................... **Fourth** (4ᵗʰ) Means **4**

**Fifth** (5ᵗʰ) Means **5** .................... **Sixth** (6ᵗʰ) Means **6**

# The Alphabet

## How Words Are Created

Words are created by putting letters of the alphabet together. Some words have many letters.

Example

**mosquito**

Some words have fewer letters.

Example

**mat**

"I can create a word by putting letters together. Just try it!"

**FIGURE 1-11 A picture of a student writing on a floorboard**

Learn to put letters of the alphabet together.

If you do, you will be able to create many words.

Just ask your teacher to help you.

# Chapter 1

## THE 26 LETTERS OF THE ALPHABET: HOW THEY FORM WORDS

H is the eighth (8th) letter of the alphabet.

H is for **Hat**.  light blue arrow ➡

FIGURE 1-12a man's hat

You wear a hat on your head.

There are two kinds of hats, men's hats and women's hats.

FIGURE 1-12b woman's hat

I is the ninth (9th) letter of the alphabet.

I is for **Iron**.  brown arrow ➡

FIGURE 1-13a Coal Iron

Pressing irons get very hot.
Irons help get wrinkles out of our clothes.

FIGURE 1-13b Electric Iron

GRADE 1 LANGUAGE ARTS

# The Alphabet

## THE 26 LETTERS OF THE ALPHABET: HOW THEY FORM WORDS

**J** is the tenth (10th) letter of the alphabet.

**J** is for **Jar**.

A jar holds many things.

We keep cookies and candies inside a jar.

**FIGURE 1-14** Picture of a cookie jar

**K** is the eleventh (11th) letter of the alphabet.

**K** is for **Kola**.

Kola nuts grow on trees in Africa.

People eat kola nuts to keep them awake.

What other things do people do with kola nuts?

**FIGURE 1-15** Picture of Kola nuts. Kola nuts grow on trees in Africa

# Chapter 1

## THE 26 LETTERS OF THE ALPHABET: HOW THEY FORM WORDS

L is the twelfth (12th) letter of the alphabet.

L is for **Lion**. → silver arrow

FIGURE 1-16 Picture of an African Lion. Lion is King of the Jungle

Lions live in the bush.

A lion is a very big cat that eats animals.

M is the thirteenth (13th) letter of the alphabet.

M is for **Mouse**. → lime green arrow

FIGURE 1-17 Picture of a mouse, commonly known in Liberia as rat

Mice (plural) make people sick.

Mice live in bushes and in our homes.

Where are the other places that mice live?

GRADE 1 LANGUAGE ARTS

# The Alphabet

## THE 26 LETTERS OF THE ALPHABET: HOW THEY FORM WORDS

N is the fourteenth (14th) letter of the alphabet.

**N** is for **Nail**. → blue arrow

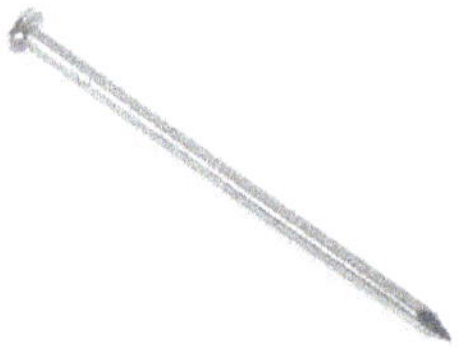

Nails are made of steel or plastic.

**Nails are used to hold things together.**

FIGURE 1-18 Picture of a nail. Nails are used by a carpenter

O is the fifteenth (15th) letter of the Alphabet.

**O** is for Orange. → purple arrow

Oranges grow on trees.

Orange are fruits that grow on Orange trees.

**Oranges come from the flowers made by the orange trees.**

FIGURE 1-19 Picture of an orange. Oranges grow from flowers made by the Orange tree

# Chapter 1

## WHAT HAVE WE LEARNED SO FAR? PUTTING IT ALL TOGETHER

### Vocabulary

1. Hat
2. Iron
3. Jar
4. Kola
5. Lion
6. Mouse
7. Nail
8. Orange

### Sequences and Numbers

**Seventh** (7th) Means **7** .................... **Eighth** (8th) Means **8**

**Ninth** (9th) Means **9** ....................... **Tenth** (10th) Means **10**

**Eleventh** (11th) Means **11** ................ **Twelfth** (12th) Means **12**

GRADE 1 LANGUAGE ARTS

# The Alphabet

## How Words Are Created

Words are created by combining groups of letters.

Some words sound the same, but are spelled differently.

>Example: **two,** and **too**.

Other words are spelled differently, but mean the same.

>Example: **cry,** and **sob**

> Words that sound the same but are spelled differently are called homophones.

FIGURE 1-20 A picture of a student reading

Learn to combine letters of the alphabet.

If practice, you will also learn how to read and write better.

Just ask your teacher to help you.

# Chapter 1

**THE 26 LETTERS OF THE ALPHABET: HOW THEY FORM WORDS**

**P** is the Sixteenth (16th) letter of the alphabet.

# P is for **Peanut**. →red arrow→

Peanuts grow under the ground.
We eat parched peanuts and boiled peanuts.
**Peanuts** are also called ground peas in Liberia.

FIGURE 1-21 Picture of peanuts or ground peas as they are referred to in Liberia

**Q** is the Seventeenth (17th) letter of the Alphabet.

# Q is for **Queen**. →yellow arrow→

A queen is a female.
A queen is a wife of a king.
**Nefertiti** was a beautiful queen from Egypt.
Egypt is a country found in East Africa.

FIGURE 1-22 Picture of Queen Nefertiti, the most beautiful queen of Egypt

# The Alphabet

## THE 26 LETTERS OF THE ALPHABET: HOW THEY FORM WORDS

R is the Eighteenth (18th) letter of the alphabet.

R is for **Ruler**.

**FIGURE 1-23** Picture of a ruler which is made of wood. Ruler measure the lengths of things

**Rulers are used to measure the length of things.**

A ruler can be made of wood or plastic.

A ruler is used to measure things in the classroom.

What are the other things you do with a ruler?

S is the Nineteenth (19th) letter of the alphabet.

S is for **Star**.

**A star has five corners.**

**FIGURE 1-24** Picture of a star. Our flag has a white star on it.

The Liberian flag has one star on it.

The Liberian flag is called the Lone Star.

Why do we call the Liberian flag the Lone Star?

# Chapter 1

**THE 26 LETTERS OF THE ALPHABET: HOW THEY FORM WORDS**

**T** is the Twentieth (20th) letter of the tlphabet.

# T is for **Turtle**. → orange arrow

FIGURE 1-25 Picture of a turtle. Turtles live in a hard outer shell

**Turtles have four legs.**
Turtles have a hard outer shell they live in.
A turtle eats grass and bugs for food.

**U** is the Twenty-first (21st) letter of the alphabet.

# U is for **Umbrella**. → light blue arrow

FIGURE 1-26 Picture of an umbrella. Umbrellas help protect people from the rain and sun

**Umbrellas help to protect us from the sun and rain.**
Umbrellas can be made of cloth or plastic.
Umbrellas come in many different colors.

# The Alphabets

## WHAT HAVE WE LEARNED SO FAR? PUTTING IT ALL TOGETHER

### Vocabulary

1. Peanuts

2. Queen

3. Ruler

4. Star

5. Turtle

6. Umbrella

### Sequences and Numbers

**Thirteenth** (13th) Means **13**..............**Fourteenth** (14th) Means **14**

**Fifteenth** (15th) Means **15**..................**Sixteenth** (16th) Means **16**

**Seventeenth** (17th) Means **17**...........**Eighteenth** (18th) Means **18**

**Ninth** (19th) Means **19**........................**Twentieth** (20th) Means **20**

# Chapter 1

## How Words Are Created

**Words are created by mixing letters of the alphabet.**

Some words make you happy.

>  Example: **smile,** or **laugh**.

>  > Other words make you sad.

>  >  Example: **hungry,** or **sick**.

> Words have power. Some words can make you happy or make you sad.

**FIGURE 1-27 A picture of students in English class**

Learn to mix letters of the alphabet to form words.

If practice, you will build your vocabulary or reading skills.

Just ask your teacher to help you.

# The Alphabet

## THE 26 LETTERS OF THE ALPHABET: HOW THEY FORM WORDS

**V** is the Twenty-second (22nd) letter of the alphabet.

**V** is for **Van**.  →purple arrow→

FIGURE 1-28 A picture of a van. A van is able to carry a lot of people or goods

**A Van is a vehicle used for transporting people or goods.**

Vans are able to carry more than six people. A motor vehicle has an engine and tires.

**W** is the Twenty-third (23rd) letter of the alphabet.

**W** is for **Water**.  →orange arrow→

FIGURE 1-29 A picture of children drinking water at a hand pump in Liberia

Water is required for life. Every living thing needs water to stay alive. Plants and animals drink water everyday.

# Chapter 1

**THE 26 LETTERS OF THE ALPHABET: HOW THEY FORM WORDS**

**X** is the Twenty-fourth (24th) letter of the alphabet.

**X** is for **X-ray**.

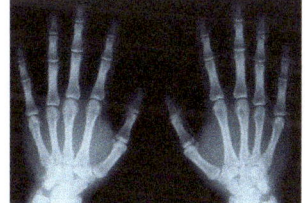

FIGURE 1-30 Picture of an X Ray of a human hand

An X-ray is a light.

An X-ray sees the inside of things.

An X-ray lets doctors see inside a person's body.

**Y** is the Twenty-fifth (25th) letter of the alphabet.

**Y** is for **Yam**.

FIGURE 1-31 A picture of two yam tuber. Yams grow under the soil

Yams grow under the soil in tube form.

A yam is a food we cook or fry to eat.

Yams and cassavas almost look the same.

# The Alphabet

## The 26 letters of the Alphabet: How they form words

Z is the Twenty-sixth (26th) letter of the alphabet.

**Z** is for **Zoo**. ⟶ red arrow

FIGURE 1-32 Picture of Charles Steiner caring for the animals at the Lakpazee zoo in Monrovia in 1977

A **zoo** is a park where different animals are kept for people to see.

Children go to the zoo to see animals.
A zookeeper cares for the animals.

Z is the Twenty-sixth (26th) letter of the alphabet.

**Z** is also for **Zebra**. ⟶ yellow arrow

FIGURE 1-33 Picture of a zebra in the Serengeti National Park in Tanzania, in East Africa

A Zebra is an animal.
Zebras live in the wild and eat grass.
Zebras have black and white stripes.

# Chapter 1 Review

**WHAT HAVE WE LEARNED SO FAR? PUTTING IT ALL TOGETHER**

## Vocabulary

1. Van
2. Water
3. X-ray
4. Yam
5. Zoo
6. Zebra

## Sequences and Numbers

**Twenty-first** (21$^{st}$) Means **21**....**Twenty-second** (22$^{nd}$) Means **22**

**Twenty-third** (23$^{rd}$) Means **23**..**Twenty-fourth** (24$^{th}$) Means **24**

**Twenty-fifth** (25$^{th}$) Means **25**......**Twenty-sixth** (26$^{th}$) Means **26**

# Chapter 1 Review

## LET'S FIND OUT

**Write the correct name next to the picture**

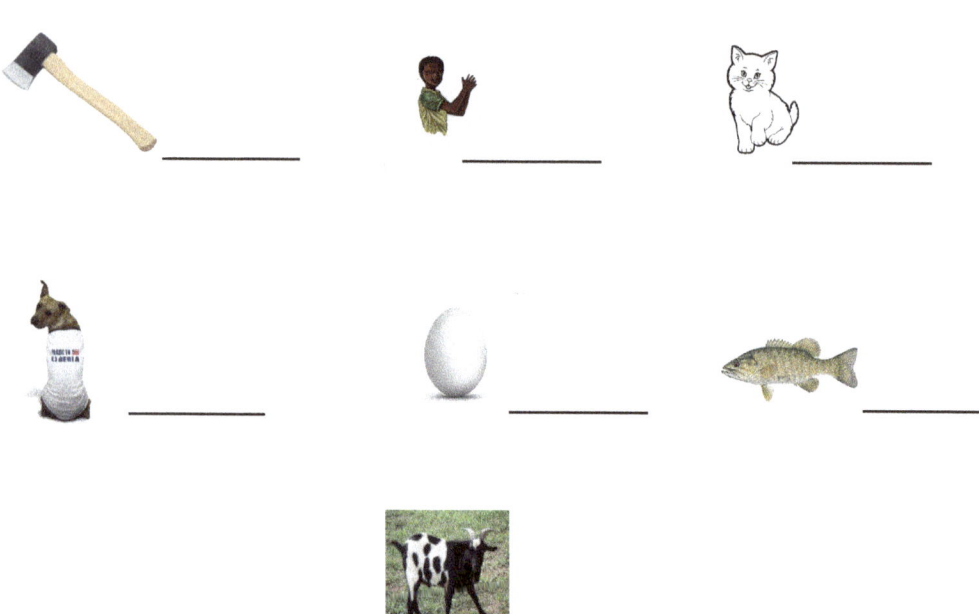

**Connecting words with meanings**

1. It is used to cut down big trees. _____

2. It eats grass or cassava leaves. _____

3. We fry or boil it to eat. _____

4. It lives underwater. _____

5. A male child. _____

6. It lives in our homes. _____

7. It is man's best friend. _____

First means? _____
Second means? _____
Third means? _____
Fourth means? _____
Fifth means? _____
Sixth means _____
Seventh means? _____

# Chapter 1 Review

## LET'S FIND OUT

**Write the correct name next to the picture**

 _____     _____     _____

 _____     _____     _____

 _____     _____

**Connecting words with meaning**

1. You wear it on your head. _____
2. It removes wrinkles. _____
3. It stores cookies. _____
4. It is very bitter. _____
5. It is king of the jungle. _____
6. It makes people sick. _____
7. It holds things together. _____
8. It is very sweet. _____

Eighth means? _____
Ninth means? _____
Tenth means? _____
Eleventh means? _____
Twelfth means? _____
Thirteenth means _____
Fourteenth means? _____
Fifteenth means? _____

# Chapter 1 Review

## LET'S FIND OUT

**Write the correct name next to the picture**

 _____    _____    _____

 _____    _____    _____

### Connecting words with meanings

1. It grows underground. _____
2. The wife of a king. _____
3. Used in the classroom to measure things. _____
4. It shines in the sky at night. _____
5. It lives in a hard shell. _____
6. It protects you from the rain or the sun. _____

Sixteenth means? _____

Seventh means? _____

Eighteenth means? _____

Nineteenth means? _____

Twentieth means? _____

Twenty-first means? _____

# Chapter 1 Review

## LET'S FIND OUT

**Write the correct name next to the picture**

 _____    _____    _____

 _____    _____

### Connecting words with meanings

1. It carries a lot of people. _____
2. You drink it everyday. _____
3. It looks inside of you. _____
4. It grows underground. _____
5. It has black & white strips. _____

Twenty-second means? _____

Twenty-third means? _____

Twenty-fourth means? _____

Twenty-fifth means? _____

Twentieth-six means? _____

REVIEW

Next Chapter

# CHAPTER TWO OBJECTIVES

How to Treat Others ........30
The Golden Rules ............30
Dos and Don'ts ............31
Basic Greetings .................32
How to Greet Others .....33
Naming Words .................34
Nouns ...........................34
Proper Nouns ................35
The Eight Parts of Speech.37
Nouns ...........................38
Singular Nouns .............39

# Courtesy And Respect

## Courtesy and Respect: How to Treat Others

**Courtesy** is to be polite to other people.

### Example:

Always raise your hand if you want to ask a question in class.

**Respect** is to show regard for other people or the law.

### Example:

Always keep quiet when the teacher is teaching class.

FIGURE 2-1 A picture of a student talking about courtesy

"It is always good to introduce or show your name to new people."

FIGURE 2-2 Picture of a student also speaking about courtesy

"Everybody has a name. Can you please introduce yourself to the class?"

# Chapter 2

## Courtesy and Respect: How to Treat Others

**The Golden Rules of Courtesy and Respect**
Treat other people the same way you like them to treat you.

| DOs | DON'Ts |
|---|---|
| Always be positive. | Say negative things. |
| Greet people whenever you enter a room with people. | Enter a room filled with people without greeting them. |
| Always respect people that are older than you. | Disrespect your elders or older people. |
| When an older person needs help, please help them. | Turn your back on a person that needs your help. |
| Respect your friends always. | Disrespect your friends. |
| Feed people that are hungry when you have enough to eat. | Leave a person hungry if you have enough food. |
| Be honest always, even if other people are not. | Take part in cheating or stealing. Be honest always! |
| Show love and kindness to your family, friends and everyone in your community. | Be mean or wicked to your family, friends and people in your neighborhood. |
| Respect your teacher and always pay attention in class whenever he or she teaches. | Ever disrespect your teacher or disturb the class when he or she is teaching. |
| Always put Liberia first because without you, there will be no country called Liberia. | Partake in illegal or immoral act that will destroy Liberia and your good name. |

# Greetings

## Basic Greetings: How to Treat Others

**Good morning** should be the first words you say to your parents when you wake up from bed in the morning.

**Good morning** must be the first words you tell your teacher when you enter the classroom in the morning.

**Good morning** are the first words you say to your friends when you meet them in the morning.

FIGURE 2-3 Picture of students in class greeting each other

# Chapter 2

## BASIC GREETINGS: HOW TO TREAT OTHERS

Whenever someone greets you, always greet them back.

Always use proper English whenever you respond.

Avoid speaking colloquial or broken Liberian English.

| Say | Don't Say |
|---|---|
| Good morning Ms. Kollie. | Morning Ms. Kollie. |
| Good afternoon papa. | Hello papa. |
| My name is Peter. | My name Peter. |
| I am going to school. | I going to school. |
| I am seven years old. | I seven year old. |
| Come let us eat. | Come let eat. |
| Is your mother home? | Your ma home? |
| Miatta is my best friend. | Miatta that my best friend. |

*What you say matters!*

Always learn to speak proper English whenever you're in school or with family, friends and strangers. Those who speak proper English are well respected.

GRADE 1 LANGUAGE ARTS

# Naming Words

## NAMING WORDS: HELP US IDENTIFY THINGS

Naming Words are very important.

They are words we give to.......

things, people, animals and places.

**A Naming Word is also called a Noun.**

Examples:

| Things | People | Animals | Places |
|--------|--------|---------|--------|
| Apple  | Abel   | Ant     | Liberia |
| Book   | Betty  | Bat     | Ghana  |
| Mat    | Kemah  | Deer    | Monrovia |
| Pen    | Mamie  | Rat     | Gbondoi |
| Pencil | Paul   | Rooster | Kakata |
| Table  | Sekou  | Sheep   | Nimba  |

A Noun is part of the Eight Parts of Speech. A noun is the name of a person, an animal, a place, or a thing.

FIGURE 2-4 Picture of a student also telling us about a noun

# Chapter 2

## NAMING WORDS: HELP US IDENTIFY THINGS

Some Naming Words are special names like, your name and my name.

Some special names include the names of people and places.

**Special names are called Proper Nouns.**

These special names always begin with Capital Letters.

### Examples:

**Emmanuel Clarke**   **Kakata**   **Liberia**   **Harbel Firestone**

Girl is not a special name.

Dog is not a special name.

**FIGURE 2-5** Picture of a girl and her dog

# Naming Words

## Naming Words: Help Us Identify Things

The names of every elderly person has a title.

**A Title is a word that comes before the name of a person.**

It is always good to call an elderly person by his or her title.

In Liberia, most adults love being called by their titles and not by their names.

Some examples of titles are: Mr. Saye, Mrs. Brown, Ms. Bah, Dr. Herring, Pastor Freeman, Honorable Flomo, etc.

FIGURE 2-6 Picture of people in a meeting.

# Chapter 2

## NAMING WORDS AND THE PARTS OF SPEECH

FIGURE 2-7 A collage of some Naming Words along with some Special Naming Words. Can you identify some of the words in this collage?

**All Naming Words are part of the Eight Parts of Speech.**

The Eight Parts of Speech are eight groups of words that help students write, read, and speak proper English.

### The Eight Parts of Speech are:

1. Noun
2. Pronoun
3. Verb
4. Adverb
5. Adjective
6. Preposition
7. Conjunction
8. Interjection

➤ **The Eight Parts of Speech help us learn good English.**

# Eight Parts of Speech

## The Eight Parts of Speech: An Overview

A **Noun** is the name of a person, an animal, a place, a thing, or an idea.

**Examples:**

**John** = is the name of a person.

**Dog** = is the name of a type of animal.

**Gbarnga** = is the name of a place in Liberia.

**Fufu** = is the name of a thing or food.

**Happy** = is a word for an idea.

There are many types of nouns in English Grammar. A singular noun is one of them.

FIGURE 2-8 A picture of a student with her puppy. The word puppy is a singular noun. Singular means one

# Chapter 2

## THE EIGHT PARTS OF SPEECH: NOUN-SINGULAR NOUN

**A Singular Noun** is a noun that names one person, animal, place, thing or idea.

**Examples:**

**Boy** = singular for one male child.

**Rabbit** = singular for one animal.

**City** = singular noun for one place.

**Car** = singular noun for one thing.

**Love** = singular noun for one idea.

**A Singular noun** does not have 'S' at the end of the word.

### A Poem About Singular Nouns

A word that means one
 Is a singular noun
  Even a word like phone
   Without the (s)
    Is a singular noun.
Let me hear you name
 More singular nouns
  If you can name singular nouns
   Raise up a cup.............by E.S. Clarke

GRADE 1 LANGUAGE ARTS

# Chapter 2 Review

## WHAT HAVE WE LEARNED SO FAR? PUTTING IT ALL TOGETHER

Courtesy ▶

Respect ▶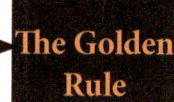

Listen to your teacher when he or she is teaching ▶

The Golden Rule helps us to be good at all times ▶ **The Golden Rule**

### Naming Words

Naming Words help us name many things, people, animals, and ideas.

Special Naming Words name special things and people.

Naming Words are part of the Eight Parts of Speech.

Titles are special names we give to adults.

A Singular Noun names only one person, animal, thing, place, or idea.

# Chapter 2 Review

## LET'S FIND OUT

**Please follow the instructions and answer all questions.**

Write T for the True statement and F for the False statement.

1. Courtesy is to be rude to others. T/F _____

2. Respect is to have regard for others and the law. T/F _____

3. Recite 5 of the Golden Rules of Courtesy and Respect.

4. What do you say to people in the morning? _____

5. When someone greets you, you do not greet them. T/F_____

6. Always use proper Liberian English in response. T/F_____

7. Always speak proper English when with friends. T/F_____

8. What are Naming Words called?_____

# Chapter 2 Review

## LET'S FIND OUT

9. Put the following Naming Words in the correct categories:

a) Liberia, b) rat, c) Fallah, d) Ghana, e) deer, f) book, g) bat, h) Paul, i) Buchanan, j) Gorpu, k) Table, l) blackboard

| Things | People | Animals | Places |
|--------|--------|---------|--------|
| _____  | _____  | _____   | _____  |
| _____  | _____  | _____   | _____  |
| _____  | _____  | _____   | _____  |

10. Special Naming Words are called what? _____

11. Title is a word that comes after people's names. T/F ____

12. Mr. Wolo is a title for a woman. T/F ____

13. Mrs. Clarke is a title for a man. T/F ____

14. Most adults in Liberia love being called by titles. T/F ____

15. All Naming Words are not part of the Eight Parts of Speech. T/F ____

16. The Eight Parts of Speech are:

   1. _____   2. _____   3. _____

# Chapter 2 Review

## LET'S FIND OUT

4. _____   5. _____   6. _____

7. _____   8. _____

17. The name of a person, animal, place, thing, or idea is called? _____

18. Give an example for each of the following nouns;

    1) person._____   2) animal._____   3) place._____

    4) thing. _____   5) idea._____

19. A Singular noun is a noun that names only one person, animal, place, or thing. T/F _____

20. Give examples of the following Singular Nouns:

    1) person _____   2) animal _____   3) place _____

    4) thing _____   5) idea _____

REVIEW

Next Chapter

# CHAPTER THREE OBJECTIVES

The Parts of Speech ..........46
Plural Noun ........................46
Verbs ...................................48
Sentence .............................48
Verb-to-Be .........................49
Helping Verb ....................52
Linking Verb ....................53
Preposition ........................54
Declarative Sentence .....57
Imperative Sentence ....58
End Marks .........................60
Period ..................................60
Question Mark ..............60
Exclamation Mark ........60

# Eight Parts of Speech

## THE EIGHT PARTS OF SPEECH: NOUN-PLURAL NOUNS

A **Plural Noun** is a noun that names more than one person, animal, place, thing or idea.

Most plural nouns end with an 's' at the end of the word.

### Examples:

**Boys** = plural for two or more male child.

**Rabbits** = plural for two or more animal.

**cars** = plural noun for many vehicles.

Some plural nouns are written differently. In fact, plural nouns are sometimes very difficult for a first grader, but your teacher and I will help you better understand them.

### Examples:

| Singular Noun Form | Plural Noun Form |
|---|---|
| Church | Churches |
| City | Cities |
| Wife | Wives |
| Oasis | Oases |
| Quiz | Quizzes |
| Zero | Zeroes |

Plural nouns can be very tricky at times because they often take many different forms.

# Chapter 3

## SOME RULES FOR PLURAL NOUNS

While the plural of most nouns is formed by adding an 's' at the end of the word, there are a few exceptions to this rule.

Below are some rules and examples of forming plurals for some nouns.

| Type of noun | Rule for Forming the Plural | Examples | Exceptions |
|---|---|---|---|
| Word ending in s, x, ch, or sh | Add 'es' to the end | ax/axes, church/churches, bus/buses, wish/wishes, trash/trashes, fox/foxes | axis/axes, ox/oxen |
| Word ending in z | Add 'zes' to the end | buzz/buzzes, quiz/quizzes | |
| Word ending in 'y' preceded by a vowel | Add 's' to the end | key/keys, play/plays, toy/toys, tray/trays, ray/rays, boy/boys, valley/valleys, | |
| Word ending in 'y' preceded by a consonant | Change the 'y' to 'ies' | army/armies, baby/babies, beauty/beauties, city/cities, party/parties, lady/ladies, try/tries, | |
| Word ending with 'f, or fe' | Change the 'f' or 'fe' to 'ves' | knife/knives, leaf/leaves, life/lives, wife/wives, wolf/wolves, loaf/loaves, | belief/beliefs, chef/chefs, safe/safes, roof/roofs |
| Ends with 'o' | Add 'es' | mosquito/mosquitoes, | zoo/zoos, |
| Ends with 'us' | Change final 'us' to 'i' | alumnus/alumni, locus/loci, syllabus/syllabi, cactus/cacti | abacus/abacuses octopus/octopuses, |

GRADE 1 LANGUAGE ARTS

# Eight Parts of Speech

## The Eight Parts of Speech: Verb-verb to be

A **Verb** is an action word.

**Examples:**

run, laugh, cry, dance, drink, buy, fight, drive, beat, bring, eat.

A verb tells you what someone or something does.

**Examples:**

1) John <u>runs</u> very fast.  2) Lorpu <u>eats</u> dry rice and fried fish.

The **subject** is what a sentence talks about.

**Examples:**

1. <u>John</u> = is the subject in the first sentence.
2. Lorpu = is the subject of the second sentence.

A **Sentence** is a group of words that makes a complete thought.

**Examples:**

1) Liberia has fifteen counties.  2) My parents really love me.

Verb is the most important part of the Eight Parts of Speech

# Chapter 3

## THE EIGHT PARTS OF SPEECH: VERB-VERB TO BE

The **Verb-To-Be** talks about what a person or a group of people are doing in a sentence.

The **verb-to-be** can be very hard to understand at times because it takes many different forms.

**Examples:**

| am | I **am** going to school. |
| --- | --- |
| is | He **is** coming from Nimba. |
| are | You **are** going to respect the teacher. |
| was | She **was** the president or our class. |
| were | You **were** at the playground yesterday. |

Why do they call it verb to be?

Because it is a verb that talks about what a person is doing. Like what we are doing now.

FIGURE 3-1 Picture of students in the village discussing the verb-to-be

GRADE 1 LANGUAGE ARTS

# Eight Parts of Speech

## The Eight Parts of Speech: Verbs-verb to be

We learned that a verb is an action word.

Do you know how to spot a verb in a sentence?

It is not hard because the verb always shows action.

Look at the pictures and tell your teacher what is happening.

FIGURE 3-2 Picture of a mother and child

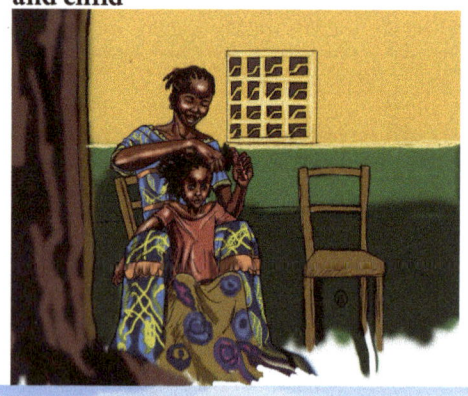

FIGURE 3-3 Picture of a brother and sister

Can you explain what is going on in these three pictures?

Have your teacher help you.

FIGURE 3-4 Picture of neighborhood boys

# Chapter 3

## THE EIGHT PARTS OF SPEECH: VERB-verb to be

To spot the verb in a sentence always ask this question.

What is the subject doing?

**Example:**

Mardea is walking to school.

Now, let us ask the sentence this question.

**Question: What is Mardea doing?**

**Answer: Walking**

You see, walking shows an action, therefore it is the verb.

*A quick look at subject*

On the other hand, to spot the subject in a sentence, you can also ask the sentence this question.

Who? or What? is doing something?

**Example:**

Mardea is walking to school.

Now, let us ask the sentence this question.

**Question: Who is walking to school?**

**Answer: Mardea**

Here, Mardea is doing something, therefore she is the subject.

# Eight Parts of Speech

**WHAT HAVE WE LEARNED SO FAR? PUTTING IT ALL TOGETHER**

**Plural Nouns** ➤ name more than one noun

**Verb** ➤ an action word

**Subject** ➤ main idea in a sentence

**Verb-to-be** ➤ verb about a person

**How spot a verb** ➤ ask the question "what"

**How to spot subject** ➤ ask the question "how"

## Tips for Plural Nouns

1. Add 's' to the end of most nouns to form their plurals.
2. Nouns like data, media, sheep, do not have plurals.

## Tips for verbs

1. A verb can be a helping verb or a linking verb.

A **Helping verb** is a verb that helps a noun in a sentence.

**Examples:** is, are, has, have, can, could, may, might, been, etc.

A **Linking verb** links a noun to the subject in a sentence.

# Chapter 3

## What have we learned so far? Putting it all together

### Nouns in picture and practice

Identify each noun and write a complete sentence about it.

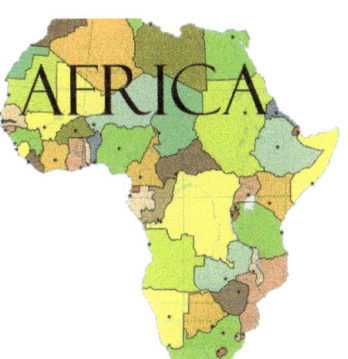

# Eight Parts of Speech

## THE EIGHT PARTS OF SPEECH: PREPOSITIONS

Preposition is like a bodyguard to a noun.

You could also say, a preposition is like a child and a parent living in a home.

When someone comes to visit the home, the child answers the door.

A **Preposition** is a word that comes after a noun.

A proposition links a noun to other words in a sentence

**A preposition shows the relationship between a noun and other words in a sentence.**

**A preposition shows time or location in a sentence.**

FIGURE 3-5 Picture of a student talking about prepositions.

**Example:**

The book is **on** the table.

The preposition **on** shows where the book is located.

54

# Chapter 3

## THE EIGHT PARTS OF SPEECH: PREPOSITIONS

Below are some examples of prepositions. Can you think of other kinds of prepositions?

| Preposition | Type | Example |
|---|---|---|
| at | time | Papa comes home **at** night. |
| ago | time | Kulah got married two years **ago**. |
| for | time | I lived in Kakata **for** two years. |
| by | time | Mom will be back **by** 1 o'clock. |
| in | place | Alex is **in** a yellow taxi. |
| under | place | The book is **under** the table. |
| over | place | The man jumped **over** the fence. |
| from | place | We bought cassava **from** the market. |

A preposition helps us better understand a sentence.

A preposition helps us connect the dots in a sentence.

**A preposition shows us the time or the place an event takes place.**

Example:

Boimah is on a holiday **until** Wednesday, September 29.

**A preposition shows us the location of things.**

Example:

Jenebah is standing **beside** the black car.

# The Parts of a Sentence

## Sentences and The Parts of a Sentence

Remember we learned that a sentence is a group of words that make a complete thought.

Every sentence must begin with a capital letter.

Every sentence must always end with an end mark.

**Example:**

Siah is studying her lesson for the English test.

A sentence has two main parts:

1. Subject
2. Predicate

The **Subject** tells us what the sentence is about.

**Example:**

**Arku** likes to play football.

This sentence is telling us that **Arku** likes to play football.

The **Predicate** tells us what is happening in the sentence.

**Example:**

**Watta** and **Favor** are playing knock foot.

Here we know that **Watta** and **Favor** are playing knock foot.

*A sentence comes in many forms or types.*

# Chapter 3

## SENTENCES AND THE TYPES OF SENTENCES

There are four (4) types of sentences in the English Language.

**1. Declarative Sentence**

**2. Imperative Sentence**

**3. Exclamatory Sentence**

**4. Interrogative Sentence**

If you learn these four different kinds of sentences, you will be a better English speaker and writer.

### Example:

A **Declarative Sentence** makes a statement.

A declarative sentence is the most important sentence in the English Language. It ends with a period (.) mark.

You will spend most of your time making statements.

### Examples:

Ellen is my classmate, and she is eight years old.

Zoe goes to Grand Gedeh for every summer vacation.

Wleh and Tannie live in Barclayville, Grand Kru County.

# The Types of Sentences

## Sentences and The Types of Sentences

A policeman always uses commands to stop moving cars.

**An Imperative Sentence gives a command or makes a polite request for something.**

**Police officers and soldiers use a lot of imperative sentences on the job. It ends with a period (.) or exclamation (!) mark.**

### Examples:

1. Get out of the way, the truck is coming!

2. Please get out of the way, the truck is coming.

3. Give me that bowl, so I can fix my Fufu and soup.

FIGURE 3-6
Picture of teacher and students in English class

# Chapter 3

## SENTENCES AND THE TYPES OF SENTENCES

Hey!, Ouch! WOW! Look! snake! These words show strong emotions or feelings. They are parts of exclamatory words.

**An Exclamatory Sentence expresses strong feelings or excitement.**

Exclamatory sentences always end with an Exclamation (!) Mark. The sirens from a fire truck or an ambulance are like exclamation marks because they bring strong emotions.

### Example:

Get out of the way, the truck is coming!

### Example:

**An Interrogative Sentence asks a question.**

**The interrogative sentence is the second most used sentence in the English Language. It always ends with a question (?) mark.**

### Examples:

1. What is your name?

2. Where do you live?

3. How are you feeling today, Miatta?

# The Types of Sentences

## Punctuation or End Marks

**An end mark or punctuation mark brings a sentence to an end.**

There are three (3) main end marks in the English Language.

1. Period (.)
2. Question mark (?)
3. Exclamation mark (!)

**Example:**

**A Period ends a statement or a command sentence.**

**Examples:**

1. I am going to the Executive Mansion to see the President.
2. Put the palm nuts into the big pot.

**Example:**

**A Question mark ends a question sentence.**

**Example:**

What school do you attend?

**An Exclamation mark ends an exclamatory sentence.**

**Example:**

The house is on fire!

*Always make it a habit to put an end mark at the end of a sentence.*
*Without an end mark, a sentence is incomplete.*

# Chapter 3

**WHAT HAVE WE LEARNED SO FAR? PUTTING IT ALL TOGETHER**

Preposition ➤ Shows time or location

- Preposition of time ➤ We go to sleep at night.
- Preposition of location ➤ The Kool Aid is on the table.

Sentence ➤ Makes a complete thought

Declarative ➤ Makes a statement

Imperative ➤ Gives a command

Exclamatory ➤ Expresses a strong feeling

Interrogative ➤ Asks a question

End mark ➤ Brings a sentence to an end.

Period ➤ (.)

Question mark ➤ (?)

Exclamatory mark ➤ (!)

# Reading: Poem/Story

## Poem and Story Time: Reading Comprehension

### The Man And The King

A man name Dan
Who came from Veahn
To demand his man
From the mean king, Ben
Who lives in a den.

The king was mean
To the man named Dan
Who never had a fear
For the ugly bear Beer
Dan never feared Ben and Beer..by ES. Clarke

### The Story of Nuumba: The Boy Who Dreams....by ES Clarke

Deep in the forest of Guata in River Cess County, there lived a boy named Nuumba.

Nuumba was 11 years old, but had never been to school. Like every child, he wanted to go to school, but he could not.

He lived with his grandmother who was ill from a disease called River Blindness. Nuumba had lost both parents in a motor vehicle accident on the Buchanan and Monrovia Highway when he was just six years old.

His grandmother had also lost her husband in a hunting

Story Continues On Next Page

**POEM AND STORY TIME: READING COMPREHENSION**

accident two years before taking Nuumba to raise him.

The village where Nuumba and his grandmother lived was some three hours walk from Guata, where the schools were.

One night in a dream, Nuumba saw himself in a school uniform and sitting in a classroom among other children. The next morning, little Nuumba went to his grandmother and told her these words:

"I want to go to school, grandma," he said.

The gray-haired old woman smiled faintly as she searched for words to respond to Nuumba's request.

"My child, Nuumba, I do not have any money to send you to school," she replied.

This was not the answer Nuumba wanted to hear. He fell onto the ground crying and rolling all over the dirt floor.

"Listen, my child," she pleaded with the weeping boy.

"Though I may not have the money to send you to school, it does not mean you will not go to school," she replied, as she wiped away her tears which were rolling down her cheeks.

"How am I going to take care of you when I cannot go to

# Reading: Poem/Story

## POEM AND STORY TIME: READING COMPREHENSION

*The Story of Nuumba: The Boy Who Dreams....by ES Clarke*

school, Grandma?" he asked as more tears rolled down his young cheeks. His crying was now echoing throughout the empty mud house and onto neighboring houses in the village.

"God will make a way, my child. He always does," she smiled as she gently rubbed his head.

"Come here. Tell me, what do you want to be when you grow up?" she asked, trying to give hope to her sobbing grandson.

Without giving the question much thought, he yelled out, "Doctor. I want to be a doctor, just like Dr. Josephus Bolongei at the clinic in Guata, Grandma," he said.

> Dream big and work hard because you can be anything you want to be.

FIGURE 3-7 Picture of a boy telling you to dream big. Like you or this boy, I also had a big dream of growing up and going to school to become a writer and a teacher. When I told family and friends, I was laughed at; but I never gave up on my dreams. I worked hard at realizing these dreams. This is one of them you're now reading here. Please keep dreaming!

Story Continues On Next Page

# Chapter 3

## Poem and Story Time: Reading Comprehension

"Really? That will be very good," she said.

"Look Grandma, if I become a doctor, I will help all the little children and the old people get better," he said with a joy of childish hopes and unbridled expectations in his voice.

"You know that you can be anything or anyone you want to be, right, Nuumba," she said with a question.

"Yes, I know because you are always saying it. I know I can really be a doctor but I don't know when," he replied.

"The question is not when, but will you be ready when that time comes? Try to go down the creek for drinking water, I am getting really thirsty," she rubbed his head some more.

Replacing the sobbing with smiles and giggles, Nuumba got up and took an empty plastic gallon jug and went down to the creek to fetch drinking water for his blind grandmother.

That day, Nuumba went into the nearby forest to gather wild fruits, yams, and some vegetables from the garden. While in the forest, he was nearly bitten by a poisonous black snake called "Black Mamba". Nuumba was very quick to have scared the snake away without being bitten.

Still in the village, the soon days turned into weeks, and weeks turned into months as Nuumba waited to see this God come

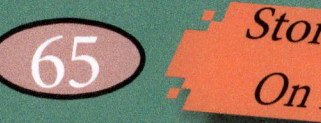

## Reading: Poem/Story

**POEM AND STORY TIME: READING COMPREHENSION**

whom his grandmother said would help him go to school.

Every night before he went to bed, he would pray to God for help in getting him to school. He would say the proudest prayer a boy could think of from the bottom of his tender and innocent heart.

He would say, "Dear God, please help me to go to school and become a doctor. If you do, I will help all the little children get better, and the old people live longer and see better. But if you do not do it, I will keep disturbing you, every hour and everyday of my life. Amen."

Two weeks before the Christmas and New Year Holidays, the local chicf in Guata, who was a family member of Nuumba's grandmother, went to get them out of the village to take them to the big city. He had gotten a job with a company in Monrovia. When Nuumba heard the news, he was glowing with joy and excitement. Wasting no time, he ran into the mud house, into his little corner and said a prayer to God.

He said, "Thank you God. I knew you were going to answer my prayers. Grandma was right about you all along!"

Do you have any story to tell the class? Please share your story with your teacher and classmates. Ask your teacher to help you learn how to write a good story.

# Chapter 3 Review

## LET'S FIND OUT

Follow the instructions and answer all questions correctly.

1. A plural noun names more than one thing T/F? _____
2. All plural nouns end with a 'z' T/F? _____
3. The plural for the following are written as follows:

    1. boy _____     2. girl _____     3. bitter ball _____
    4. coconut _____  5. city _____    6. quiz _____
    7. wolf _____    8. hero _____    9. mother _____

4. A verb is an _____
5. Write four sentences that have action verbs below:

    1. _____  2. _____
    3. _____  4. _____

6. A sentence expresses a complete thought. T/F _____
7. Write four complete sentences below:

    1. _____  2. _____
    3. _____  4. _____

8. The "verb-to-be" does not talk about people. T/F _____
9. Write the sentence and underline the verb to be in it:

    1. _____  2. _____
    3. _____  4. _____

10. To spot the verb, you ask this question? _____

# Chapter 3 Review

## LET'S FIND OUT

11. To spot the subject, you ask this question?_____

12. A Preposition is a word that comes after a noun. T/F____

13. A Preposition shows time and money. T/F____

14. Underline the preposition in the sentences below:

    1. David sleeps for nine hours everyday.

    2. Moses put the coal pot on the ground.

    3. Some people in Kla eat late at night.

    4. Mable came home from the hospital today.

15. A sentence has two main parts. T/F____

16. _____ tells us what the sentence is talking about.

17. _____ tells us what is happening in the sentence.

18. There are four kinds of sentences. T/F____

19. The four types of sentences are as follows:

    1._____  2._____
    3._____  4._____

20. Select the correct sentence by writing its name next to it.

    1. Have you eaten?          2. George is a good man.

    3. Pick up that dirt.        4. Look at the snake!

# Chapter 3 Review

## LET'S FIND OUT

**Analysis of "The Story of Nuumba: The Boy Who Dreams"**

1. Why did Nuumba have a very rough childhood?

    a. He lived in a village.
    b. His grandmother prayed for him each day.
    c. Nuumba's parents died and his grandmother had no money to send him to school.
    d. Nuumba had to go to the creek to get drinking water.

2. What did Nuumba do the morning after his dream?

    a. He told his grandmother "good morning".
    b. He told her he wanted to go to school.
    c. He told her he needed slippers to wear in the yard.
    d. He told her he wanted to visit Monrovia.

3. What did Nuumba do when his grandma said she had no money?

    a. Began crying and rolling on the dirt floor.
    b. Went into his room to sleep.
    c. Began praying to God for someone to help him.
    d. He got very mad at his grandmother.

4. What did the chief do for Nuumba and his grandmother?

    a. He sent her money to put Nuumba in school.
    b. He sent for Nuumba to come to Guata for school.
    c. He took Nuumba and his grandmother to Monrovia.

**Next Chapter**

# CHAPTER FOUR OBJECTIVES

Adjectives ................................72  Rhymes ...............................89
Describe .................................72  Poems and Story ................93
Pronoun ..................................75  Liberians and Question ....93
Demonstrative Pronouns..77  Our Journey .......................96
Personal Pronouns .......79  Beauty of Poem ................96
Numbers And Words .......81  L.I.B .....................................97

# Adjectives

## ADJECTIVES: DESCRIBING NOUNS AND PRONOUNS

**Describe means to tell how a person or a thing looks**.

Describing words can tell you something about a noun or a pronoun.

These words can tell you how big or small, how short or tall, or how pretty or ugly something is. They can also tell you the color or the smell of nouns or pronouns.

A Describing word is called an **Adjective**.

**An Adjective is a word used to describe a noun or pronoun**.

**Examples**: red, small, brave, smart, ugly, big, old, cold, new.

### Examples:

1. Pauline has a very **tall** brother.
2. What is Sando doing with that **dirty** pan?
3. Kou, look at the **big** snake!
4. She is wearing a **yellow** dress.

I think without an Adjective, we would not have known how things look.

FIGURE 4-1 Picture of a student talking about Adjectives

## ADJECTIVES: DESCRIBING NOUNS AND PRONOUNS

**Let us look at an adjective in picture.**

**FIGURE 4-2** Picture of the national flag of Liberia, called the Lone Star. Do you know anything about the flag? Please share with your classmates

This is the flag of the Republic of Liberia, our country. The flag is called the **Lone Star**.

Using adjectives in four sentences, can you describe the flag of Liberia?

1. _____
2. _____
3. _____
4. _____

# Adjectives

## ADJECTIVES: DESCRIBING NOUNS AND PRONOUNS

Let us look at some more adjectives in pictures. Can you describe things in the pictures below? Look carefully.

FIGURE 4-3 Picture of a boy and his sister. Please describe the scenes

FIGURE 4-4 Picture of Downtown Monrovia. Please describe the scenes

FIGURE 4-5 Picture of a Nikon camera. Please describe the camera features

FIGURE 4-6 Picture of a street in Sinkor, in Monrovia. Please describe the scenes

# Chapter 4

## PRONOUNS: WORDS THAT REPLACE NOUNS

A **Pronoun** is a word that we can use to replace a noun.

**Examples:**

1. <u>Emmanuel</u> is a boy. <u>**He**</u> is handsome.

2. <u>Lorpu</u> is a girl. <u>**She**</u> is very beautiful.

### Analysis

In sentence number one, Emmanuel is a name of a person.

The pronoun "**He**" replaces Emmanuel in the second part.

### Analysis

In sentence number two, Lorpu is a name of a person.

Kanay is replaced by the pronoun "**She**" in the second part.

**Without pronouns, the English Language would be dull, because we would have to keep repeating names of nouns.**

**Examples:**

John is going to school. John tells his teacher good morning. John is playing with Kemah. John is watching television.

To stop repeating John's name, the word "**He**" can be used.

> Pronouns make writing and speaking English easy.

GRADE 1 LANGUAGE ARTS

# Pronouns

## PRONOUNS: WORDS THAT REPLACE NOUNS

**Below are some examples of pronouns.**

| PRONOUNS | Pronoun as subject | Pronoun as object |
|---|---|---|
| 1st person singular | I | me |
| 2nd person singular | you | you |
| 3rd person singular | he / she / it | him / her / it |

Like it does for a person, a pronoun can also replace the name of a thing.

### Example:

The **book** is on the table. **It** is on the table.

### Analysis

In the above sentence, book is the name of a thing.

The pronoun "**It**" replaces book in the second part.

My teacher, Ms. Kollie said that Pronoun stands for Pro + Noun.

FIGURE 4-7 Picture of a student talking about pronouns. The object is the person or thing that the action affects.

# Chapter 4

## PRONOUNS: DEMONSTRATIVE PRONOUNS

A **Demonstrative pronoun** points at a specific noun or a specific pronoun.

Demonstrative pronouns are special groups of words that do the pointing at the things or nouns.

**Example:**

The words are: **this**, **that**, **these**, and **those**.

**Let us go a little deeper.**

| Demonstrative Pronoun | Functions |
|---|---|
| This | Points at object close to speaker |
| That | Points at object far from speaker |
| These | Point at objects close to speaker |
| Those | Point at objects far from speaker |

**Demonstrative pronouns do a lot of things in a sentence.**

**Example:**

<u>This</u> book in your hands was written by Emmanuel Clarke.

The word **this,** points at a <u>book</u> written by Emmanuel Clarke.

**Example:**

<u>That</u> movie was very good.

The word **that,** points to the movie.

GRADE 1 LANGUAGE ARTS

# Pronouns

## Pronouns: Demonstrative Pronouns

**Examples:**

<u>These</u> are my friends.

The word **these,** points to friends.

<u>These</u> are the books Fatu brought.

The word **these,** points at books.

**Example:**

<u>Those</u> chairs belong in the corners.

The word **those,** points to chairs.

**Another example:**

Don't get mad, <u>Those</u> are the things they do.

The word **those,** points at the things they do.

A demonstrative pronoun shows us what things are.

FIGURE 4-8 Picture of a student talking about demonstrative pronouns. What other things do you think demonstrative pronouns do?

# Chapter 4

## PRONOUNS: PERSONAL PRONOUNS

**A Personal pronoun is used in place of a person, people or things that you talk about.**

Whenever you are speaking with a friend, and do not want to call her by her name, you use a personal pronoun.

There are twelve types of personal pronouns.

They are: i, you, he, she, her, it, we, me, him, they, them, us.

| PRONOUNS | Pronoun as subject | Pronoun as object |
|---|---|---|
| 1st person singular | I | me |
| 2nd person singular | you | you |
| 3rd person singular | he<br>she<br>it | him<br>her<br>it |
| 1st person plural | we | us |
| 2nd person plural | you | you |
| 3rd person plural | they | them |

**Examples:**

1. <u>I</u> love Liberia.
2. Dad loves <u>me</u>.
3. <u>It</u> does not work.
4. Can Moses fix <u>it</u>?
5. <u>They</u> play well.
6. Jerry and Togar beat <u>them.</u>
7. <u>We</u> went home.
8. Mom drove <u>us</u>.

GRADE 1 LANGUAGE ARTS

# Pronouns

**WHAT HAVE WE LEARNED SO FAR? PUTTING IT ALL TOGETHER**

Describe ⟶ to say how a person looks

Adjective ⟶ word that describes a noun

Pronoun ⟶ word that replaces a noun.

Demonstrative Pronoun ⟶ word that points at a noun.

Personal Pronoun ⟶ word used in place of a person

The sky is blue today. ⟶ Adjective

Decontee is pretty. ⟶ Adjective

She and Kou are coming. ⟶ Pronoun (she)

He and Varmuyan are here. ⟶ Pronoun (he)

These shoes are ugly. ⟶ Demonstrative Pronoun

That man is poor. ⟶ Demonstrative Pronoun

I live in Harper. ⟶ Personal Pronoun

You are my friend. ⟶ Personal Pronoun

# Chapter 4

**NUMBERS INTO WORDS: HOW ARE THEY RELATED?**

Let Us Count and Write.

# Numbers Into Words

## Numbers Into Words: How are they related?

**Let Us Count and Write.**

One → 1
Two → 2
Three → 3
Four → 4
Five → 5
Six → 6
Seven → 7
Eight → 8
Nine → 9
Ten → 10

# Chapter 4

## NUMBERS INTO WORDS: HOW ARE THEY RELATED?

Writing numbers in sentences is very easy.

Whenever you are writing numbers into words, make sure to spell out the number.

**Example:**

Let us look at the dialogue between these two students.

**Mary:** How old are you, D-Boy?

**D-Boy:** I am nine years old.

FIGURE 4-9 Picture of two students in a dialogue. Mary has asked D-Boy about his age and he told her his age. You see, whenever you are writing a number greater than nine, you have the choice of writing the whole number out, or writing it out into words.

# Numbers Into Words

## Numbers Into Words: How are they related?

### More on numbers

If you are writing a number that is greater than nine, you should write that whole number out.

### Example

Tenneh was **15** years old in the tenth grade.

Kweme will give you **L$D20.00** for school today.

I saw **50** cars on the street an hour ago.

These are just a few ways large numbers can be written in sentences.

Do you know other ways?

Some numbers are very large to write. 175 is one of them.

FIGURE 4-10 Picture of a student talking about numbers. She is very correct, a number like 175 is a very large number. For example, it would be written as "one hundred seventy five".

# Chapter 4

**NUMBERS INTO WORDS: HOW ARE THEY RELATED?**

GRADE 1 LANGUAGE ARTS

# Numbers Into Words

**NUMBERS INTO WORDS: HOW ARE THEY RELATED?**

Let Us Count and Write.

Eleven → 11

Twelve → 12

Thirteen → 13

Fourteen → 14

Fifteen → 15

Sixteen → 16

Seventeen → 17

Eighteen → 18

Nineteen → 19

Twenty → 20

# Chapter 4

## Numbers Into Words: How are they related?

**Writing numbers in sentences.**

Like we did previously, writing numbers into words can be easy if you know how to spell the numbers.

### Examples:

Let us look at what students and people say everyday.

**Teacher:** Liberia is less than **two hundred fifty** years old.

**Market woman:** I am selling the Bitter Balls for **L$D 250.00**.

**Bus Driver:** It is more than **twenty** miles from here to Gbar.

**Passenger:** From Tower Hill to RIA, it is less than **20** miles.

**Students:** Let us draw a team of **eleven** players for the game.

**Police Officer:** I saw **11** men stealing from that yellow house.

**School Principal:** There are **thirty-five** students in each class.

**English Teacher:** We have less than **35** English books in here.

*Ten, Twenty, Thirty, Forty, Fifty, Sixty, Seventy, Eighty, Ninety, Hundred.*

# Numbers Into Words

**NUMBERS INTO WORDS: HOW ARE THEY RELATED**

Let Us Count and Write.

Ten → 10
Twenty → 20
Thirty → 30
Forty → 40
Fifty → 50
Sixty → 60
Seventy → 70
Eighty → 80
Ninety → 90
Hundred → 100

# Chapter 4

## Words That Sound The Same: Rhymes and Words

**A Rhyme** is when one or two or more words have the same ending sounds.

Rhyming makes words more fun to read.

You can make many of the nouns to rhyme.

Nouns like **ball** and **wall** rhyme.

**Fish** and **dish** are two words that rhyme.

**Bat**, **cat** and **mat** all have the same ending sounds.

*Let us look at the pictures of everyday things that rhyme.*

FIGURE 4-11 Billy Goat

Goat

FIGURE 4-12 Ear

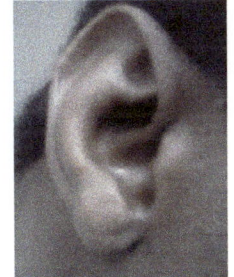

Ear

FIGURE 4-13 Potato(es)

Potato

FIGURE 4-14 Tomato(es)

Tomato

FIGURE 4-15 Boat

Boat

FIGURE 4-16 Deer

Deer

# Rhymes And Words

## Words That Sound The Same: Rhymes and Words

**Let us look at some rhyming words.**

| Hat   | Bat   |
|-------|-------|
| Tent  | Bent  |
| Ball  | Wall  |
| Trip  | Ship  |
| Duck  | Luck  |
| Fox   | Box   |
| Cat   | Rat   |
| House | Mouse |
| Hen   | Pen   |
| Ray   | Pray  |
| Braid | Maid  |
| Air   | Pair  |

**Let us use the words from the table above in a rhyme.**

1. Our house maid did my daughter's _____.
2. The cold air blew the _____ of jeans off the line.
3. The fast cat ran after the lazy gray _____.
4. The ship was brought in by men on a fishing _____.
5. The house has only one _____ trap.
6. The box was left in the woods where the _____ lives.
7. The brown hen took our teacher's red _____ from the table.
8. It was only by _____ that we found the duck.

# Chapter 4

**WHAT HAVE WE LEARNED SO FAR? PUTTING IT ALL TOGETHER**

| | |
|---|---|
| 1 | One |
| 2 | Two |
| 3 | Three |
| 4 | Four |
| 5 | Five |
| 6 | Six |
| 7 | Seven |
| 8 | Eight |
| 9 | Nine |
| 10 | Ten |
| 11 | Eleven |
| 12 | Twelve |
| 13 | Thirteen |
| 14 | Fourteen |
| 15 | Fifteen |
| 16 | Sixteen |
| 17 | Seventeen |
| 18 | Eighteen |
| 19 | Nineteen |
| 20 | Twenty |

GRADE 1 LANGUAGE ARTS

# Numbers Into Words

## What have we learned so far? Putting it all together

Ten → 10
Twenty → 20
Thirty → 30
Forty → 40
Fifty → 50
Sixty → 60
Seventy → 70
Eighty → 80
Ninety → 90
Hundred → 100

## Rhyming Words

Rhyme → Words that sound the same.

Goat → Boat

Ear → Deer

Fox → Box

Cat → Hat

Bat → Mat

# Chapter 4

## Poems and Story Time: Reading Comprehension

### Liberians Do Not Answer Questions Directly..by E.S Clarke

Deep in a faraway Turtle Land, the turtles heard that the people of Liberia did not answer questions directly.

One day, Little Turtle who was very curious, decided to leave his home deep in Turtle Land to visit Liberia.

He climbed many hills, swam across many rivers, and passed through many dangerous forests to come to Liberia.

FIGURE 4-17 Picture of Little Turtle on his journey to Liberia to find out if what he heard was true. Little turtle was very tired and hungry.

*Story Continues On Next Page*

# Reading Comprehension

## Poems and Story Time: Reading Comprehension

After traveling for six long months, Little Turtle reached the edge of a village in Lofa County.

Feeling relief to know that he had finally reached Liberia, he went down to a nearby creek in the village to take a bath and drink some fresh water.

After resting under a nearby tree and eating some fresh leaves and some bugs, Little Turtle came back to the village to find the village's chief.

He met the chief sitting in his high chair with members of his government sitting around him.

"How are you Mr. Chief? And how are you all doing today?" he greeted them politely.

FIGURE 4-18 Picture of Little Turtle in a village in Lofa as he asked the chief questions about Liberians.

"I am from Turtle Land. A place filled with beautiful turtles with kind hearts and smiling faces," the turtle said.

"I have come to ask you a question," the Little Turtle smiled.

"Ask your question, my little friend," the Chief replied.

"Is it true that Liberians do not answer questions directly, Mr. Chief?" the curious turtle asked. Everybody looked at him.

**Story Continues On Next Page**

# Chapter 4

## POEM AND STORY TIME: READING COMPREHENSION

"Who told you that we Liberians do not answer questions directly, my little friend?" the chief replied with a question.

From the chief's response, Little Turtle had his answer.

He thanked the chief for his time and went on his way to Gbarpolu County, then Bong County.

Everywhere Little Turtle went, he got the same answer from those he asked, "Who told you that we Liberians do not answer questions directly?" After visiting the fifteen counties in Liberia, he returned home to Turtle Land in the deep forest faraway. He was satisfied he had gotten the answer he had been searching for.

# Critical Thinking

**POEMS AND STORY TIME: CRITICAL THINKING**

### Our Journey to Monrovia

Our journey started in Tappita
It continues through Ganta

Monrovia the Capital of our nation

Is our final destination

As we pass through Kakata

That day we walked on Carey Street

Then we turned right on Randolph Street

I saw people walking up and down

Going all around the town.

On these very busy streets........**by Nvasekie Konneh**

### The Beauty Of Poems.....by E.S. Clarke

Poems help students to think very hard.

Poems cause students to imagine things.

Poems enable students to be creative.

Poems can be created from anything.

Poems can be found everywhere.

**These are the beauties of poems, my friends.**

# Chapter 4

**POEMS AND STORY TIME: CRITICAL THINKING**

### L.I.B.

They call it L.I.B,
 I call it the place to be
  nowhere else I'd rather be
   but right here in L.I.B.
    No matter how things may be

     I know L.I.B. is often rocky
    Sometimes even bumpy
    Hustle leaves the pressure high
   If that's the definition of pain
  I can endure it just to be in L.I.B.

Dust may fill my nostrils everyday
 I may not complain but reach for the beach
  Oh, L.I.B. how I love thee
   I can eat mango or sugarcane if I want
    Because L.I.B. is the place to be
.....................................................by Patrice Juah

**GRADE 1 LANGUAGE ARTS**

# Chapter 4 Review

## LET'S FIND OUT

Follow the instructions and answer all questions correctly.

1. Describe means to tell how a person looks. T/F _____
2. An Adjective is a word used to describe a noun. T/F _____
3. David is ugly. What is the adjective in this sentence? _____
4. A Pronoun is a word used in place of a noun. T/F _____
5. Massa is my sister. _____ is eating boiled egg and pepper.
6. A Demonstrative pronoun points at a noun. T/F _____
7. _____, _____, _____, these and _____ are demonstrative pronouns.
8. A Personal pronoun replaces a person or thing. T/F _____
9. Write from 1 to 10 in words.

   1._____, 2._____, 3._____, 4._____, 5._____, 6._____
   7._____, 8._____, 9._____, 10._____

10. Write from 11 to 20 in words.

    11._____  12._____  13._____  14._____  15._____
    16._____  17._____  18._____  19._____  20._____

11. Write the sequence of 10 to 100 in words.

    10._____, 20._____, 30._____, 40._____,
    50._____, 60._____, 70._____, 80._____,
    90._____, 100._____

# Chapter 4 Review

## LET'S FIND OUT

12. A Rhyme is for two or more words to sound alike T/F____

13. Write the word that rhymes with the following words:

    1. Hear: _____   2. Mat: _____   3. Fox: _____

    4. Wall: _____   5. Bank: _____   6. Made: _____

14. From the story we've read, do you believe that Liberians do not answer questions directly? Why or Why not?

15. Were the people in the village in Lofa County nice to Little Turtle?

16. Do you think the chief gave Little Turtle the answers he was looking for? Why or Why not?

17. How many months did Little Turtle spend on his journey to Liberia?

18. Did anybody answer Little Turtle's questions?

20. If you had been asked "Is it true Liberians do not answer questions directly," how would you have answered it?

21. If you were Little Turtle, how would you have asked the question above to the chief and the other people?

22. Do you think Little Turtle was happy when he went home to Turtle Land? Why or Why not?

REVIEW

# CHAPTER FIVE OBJECTIVES

Phonics ..................................102
Consonant Blends ............103
Action Verbs ......................106
Story Time ........................ 107
Fatu & The Blind Man.....107
Putting It All Together....111
Adjectives and Articles....112

Definite Articles ...............112
Indefinite Articles............113
Contractions......................116
Putting It All Together....119
Negative Sentences..........120
Compound Words...........122

# Phonics Time

## PHONICS TIME: VOWELS AND CONSONANTS

Before we talk about consonants and vowel sounds, we need to know what they are.

There are six vowels in the English Language Alphabet.

The vowels are: **A**, **E**, **I**, **O**, **U**, and sometimes **Y**.

The rest of the 20 letters of the alphabet are all consonants, and sometimes including '**Y**'.

Vowels and consonants are often used along with articles. We will discuss articles later in this chapter.

For you 1st graders, we will not be discussing the vowels. Instead, we will only focus on consonants blend.

Before moving onto the consonants, we need to understand what phonics is.

**Phonics shows the relationships between letters and sounds**.

### Examples:

1. **at** as in the word **Cat**.
2. **lap** as in the word **Clap**.
3. **nt** as in the word **Ant**.
4. **pple** as in the word **Apple**.
5. **ed** as in the word **Bed**.
6. **og** as in the word **Dog**.
7. **an** as in the word **Fan**.
8. **oat** as in the word **Goat**.
9. **utter** as in the word **Butter**.
10. **ox** as in the word **Fox**.

GRADE 1 LANGUAGE ARTS

# Chapter 5

## PHONICS TIME: BEGINNING CONSONANT SOUNDS

Let us look at beginning consonant blends.

**A Consonant blend is a group of consonants that appear together in a word. Each consonant is heard whenever that word is pronounced.**

### Example:

Let us look at the word "drink." Both the letters "d" and "r" are consonants. When the word "drink" is pronounced, you can clearly hear the sounds of each of these letters, making it a consonant blend.

If you learn the initial consonant combinations, you will learn to pronounce a lot of words with ease.

### Examples:

| br | cl | dr | fl | gr | pl | sc | tr | thr | scr |
|---|---|---|---|---|---|---|---|---|---|
| bread | class | drink | flag | grass | plum | school | tree | three | scrap |
| break | clap | dress | flat | great | plate | screen | truck | thread | scroll |
| brown | clock | drive | floor | grab | plug | scare | trip | thrill | scrub |
| bring | clean | dry | fly | grape | plant | score | trap | threat | scrape |

**Phonics is the key to building one's vocabulary.**

# Phonics Time

## Phonics Time: Beginning Consonant Sounds

Let us phonetically associate the below pictures with words.

# Chapter 5

## PHONICS TIME: BEGINNING CONSONANT SOUNDS

Having learned several words containing consonants, let us make new words from original words.

The new words do not have to start with the same beginning consonants.

**Examples:**

1.) I will **clap** my hands.   2.) Birds **flap** their wings to fly.

Clap = Flap

3.) I will **bring** the ball.   4.) I will not **wring** the clothes.

Bring = Wring

Let us work together to create new words.

1.) Do not **block** the road.   2.) The c_ _ck is not working.

3.) The teacher is in **class**.   4.) Mom drinks from that _ _ass.

5.) I love that blue **plate**.   6.) Dad eats from a clean _ _ate.

7.) The **frog** is in a hole.   8.) Do not _ _og the water flow.

9.) I love Fula **Bread**.   10.) S_ _ _ad the clothes out well.

---

**What you say matters.**
The way you pronounce your words and write your sentences will open or close doors unto you that you didn't know existed. Therefore, be careful of how you speak or write.

# Action Verbs

**ACTION VERB: A VERB THAT SHOWS WHAT THE SUBJECT DOES**

As stated in Chapter Three, a verb is an action word.

**An Action verb is a verb that shows an action in a sentence.**

### Examples:

1.) Run     2.) Hop     3.) Jump     4.) Clap

Everyday you use action verbs whenever you speak.

### Example:

The PE teacher wants the students to run around the school.

**Analysis:** <u>Run</u> is the action verb in this sentence.

### Below is a table containing action verbs.

| bake  | dance | feed | ride  |
|-------|-------|------|-------|
| beat  | dig   | fly  | set   |
| bite  | draw  | free | sit   |
| blow  | drink | hide | slam  |
| buy   | drop  | hop  | slap  |
| clap  | eat   | hug  | stand |
| clean | enter | mop  | step  |
| climb | erase | play | turn  |
| cook  | hear  | push | wear  |
| cut   | help  | rake | yell  |

*To know the action verb in a sentence, just close your eyes after reading a sentence. What you see in your imagination is the verb. Trust me!*

# Chapter 5

## Story Time: Reading Comprehension

### Fatu and the Tricky Blind Man.....by E.S. Clarke

In a small green house on McDonald Street, there lives a little girl by the name of Fatu. Fatu's mother, Ma Hawa has a small restaurant next to the family house on the busy street.

Ma Hawa usually cooks delicious food to sell to hungry people in the neighborhood, and to busy people that come on the street to find transport cars to get home after work or school.

The fact is, Fatu's mother is a good cook. Everybody loves her food. The little restaurant is always crowded with people.

Among the many people that came, was a blind man called John. John ate in the restaurant almost everyday until one day

FIGURE 5-13 Picture of people on a busy street in Monrovia

*Story Continues On Next Page*

### Story Time: Reading Comprehension

something happened.

This day was like any ordinary Monday. Fatu had just celebrated her thirteenth birthday that weekend. When John the Blind Man walked into the restaurant, he ordered a plate of Palaver Sauce and rice. The food tasted so good that John unknowingly ate up all the rice and tasty sauce from his plate. After the food was finished out of his plate, he kept scraping the empty plate for more food.

Ma Hawa had a lot of things in the Palava Sauce that day. The sauce had dry deer meat, crab, dry fish, cow feet, cow skin, cow meat, crayfish, dry bony fish, fresh water palm oil, the right amount of pepper, and the right amount of Vita Cube and salt. The sweet smell of the sauce reached as far as Broad Street, Ashmun Street, Capitol Bypass, and all the nearby streets around McDonald Street. The smell even reached the Capitol Building and the Executive Mansion up on Capitol Hill.

Realizing that the blind man had eaten all the food on his plate and was searching for more, Fatu slowly walked over to him, and said, "There is no more rice on the plate, my friend."

"Oh my God, how did it all disappear so quickly?" asked the blind man.

Fatu replied, "You ate everything!"

"Can you please tell your mother to credit me one more plate

# Chapter 5

## STORY TIME: READING COMPREHENSION

of rice? I will pay her tomorrow," poor John pleaded.

He waited to hear if the person would move, but he heard no movement. Five seconds passed, then ten, then a full minute.

"Did you hear me pretty little girl?" the blind man asked.

"How do you know that I am pretty, and how do you know she is my mother?" Fatu asked.

"That is easy. I can tell from the smell of your perfume and your voice sounds just like Ma Hawa," John replied.

"Okay, if you say so." Fatu sighed and continued to speak.

"Let me do this, why don't we share my food today, and when you come tomorrow, we will share yours," she suggested.

John hesitated for a little while and then slowly reached for the spoon on his empty plate.

"If you insist, I wouldn't mind," he said.

Before long, both Fatu and John were eating and having a friendly talk. After the meal, John paid for the food he ate earlier and told Fatu goodbye.

The next day, John did not show up. The days turned to weeks and weeks turned into months. Fatu was worried about the poor blind man. At times, she would go out on the streets to look for him. Soon, a year passed, then two and then three, and four years went by without seeing John, the blind man.

*Story Continues On Next Page*

# Story Time

## STORY TIME: READING COMPREHENSION

By this time, Fatu was a senior student at J.J. Roberts High School. One afternoon while going to visit a classmate of hers on Symthe Road, she heard a familiar voice of a man coming from a nearby house.

Fatu slowly walked toward the source of the voice to see if it was her long lost blind friend, John. Turning a corner, she came face-to-face with the man who she had been looking for.

"How are you, John?" she greeted him with excitement. People nearby looked on in awe as she called his name.

"My name is not John. My name is Paul," he replied.

"Stop playing, John. I have been looking for you for more than four years now," she said with outstretched hands.

"I don't know you. Please leave me alone," the man replied.

"That is okay. Now that you can see, you don't know Fatu, Ma Hawa's daughter. But when you were blind, you knew me and my mother, you tricky blind man."

When John realized that it was Fatu, the daughter of Ma Hawa, from the restaurant on McDonald Street, he dropped the bucket he had in his hand and ran between the houses.

Neighbors came and informed Fatu that John was never blind. He pretended to be blind in order to beg for help from kindhearted people in the streets. Fatu was very disappointed. She hung her head as she slowly walked to her friend's house.

# Chapter 5

## WHAT HAVE WE LEARNED SO FAR? PUTTING IT ALL TOGETHER

Vowels ━━━━━▶ A, E, I, O, U, and Y
Phonics ━━━━━▶ Shows letters' relationships
Consonants ━━━━━▶ 25 letters of the Alphabet
Initial Consonants ━━━━━▶ br, cl, dr, fl, gl, sl...
Action verbs ━━━━━▶ Verbs that show action

Circle the words that start with two consonant blends

| soon | back | drive | come |
| light | day | pet | clean |
| home | break | night | ride |
| phone | me | you | her |
| dad | why | going | peace |
| rabbit | book | school | win |

**Action verbs: Analysis of 'Fatu and the Tricky Blind Man'. Write the correct action verbs in the blank space below.**

1. Ma Hawa's food _____ very good.

2. The blind man, John _____ all the food on his plate.

3. Ma Hawa _____ very good.

4. Fatu slowly _____ toward the source of the voice.

5. The blind man, John _____ away from Fatu.

6. Fatu _____ at John with disappointment in her eyes.

# Adjectives And Articles

## Adjectives: Definite and Indefinite Articles

In the English Language, there are two types of special adjectives called **articles**.

These adjectives are: 1.) **Definite Article** 2.) **Indefinite Article**

We use a definite article if we know the things we are talking about.

Example of a Definite article is 'THE'. **A Definite Article points at or describes a thing we know or have seen before**.

### Examples:

1.) I can see the dog.   2.) The dog is black and white.

**Analysis**: The word '**The**' points at, or describes dog.

Students use definite articles every time they speak. Example: The Executive Mansion is where the President lives.

We will not focus on definite articles at this level. We will discuss more in 2nd Grade.

FIGURE 5-14 A picture of a student talking about Definite Article usage

# Chapter 5

## ADJECTIVES: INDEFINITE ARTICLES

**An Indefinite Article is a special kind of adjective that describes or points at a singular noun.**

Examples of indefinite articles are '**A**' and '**AN**'.

Use '**A**' before a noun beginning with a consonant (other than **a, e, i, o, u**).

### Examples:

1.) A mat    2.) A boy    3.) A woman    4.) A duck

### More examples:

1. My teacher Ms. Kollie is <u>a</u> woman.

2. The boy sleeps on <u>a</u> mat.

3. There is <u>a</u> duck in the pond.

4. My son C.J. is <u>a</u> boy.

Always practice using the special adjective 'A' in sentences.

Below is a table with nouns beginning with indefinite articles.

| | | | | |
|---|---|---|---|---|
| A rock | A bat | A table | A room | A school |
| A pencil | A bottle | A fish | A hand | A nose |
| A mouth | A tooth | A doctor | A team | A hand |
| A car | A house | A lion | A street | A song |
| A deer | A phone | A man | A turtle | A cassava |
| A yam | A flower | A marble | A rabbit | A wagon |

GRADE 1 LANGUAGE ARTS

# Adjectives And Articles

## ADJECTIVES: INDEFINITE ARTICLES

You should only use '**AN**' before nouns beginning with a vowel (vowels that begin with **a, e, i, o, u**).

**Examples:**

1.) An apple    2.) An elephant    3.) An eagle    4.) An ant

**More examples:**

1.) I saw Lemu eating **an** apple.

2.) Mr. Urey has **an** elephant on his farm.

3.) **An** Eagle is sitting on the tree's branch.

4.) **An** ant just crawled up on me.

Always practice using the special adjective 'AN' in sentences.

Below is a table with nouns beginning with indefinite articles.

| | | | | |
|---|---|---|---|---|
| An animal | An opener | An egg | An iron | An arrow |
| An ocean | An uncle | An eye | An uncle | An ox |
| An island | An ant | An ear | An order | An elbow |
| An aunt | An owl | An infant | An icon | An oat |
| An onion | An idol | An event | An actor | An arm |
| An echo | An igloo | An ape | An idea | An axe |

**The article 'An' should only be used with vowels.**

GRADE 1 LANGUAGE ARTS

# Chapter 5

## ADJECTIVES: DEFINITE AND INDEFINITE ARTICLES

**Let's practice by choosing the correct article in the sentences.**

1. Mulbah did not bring _____ (a, an the) umbrella today.
2. Are you looking for _____ (a, an, the) comb?
3. Papa went to _____ (a, an, the) J.F.K. Hospital today.
4. I will check _____ (a, an, the) boy's room later.
5. Look at _____ (a, an, the) Pepper Bird.
6. My daddy is _____ (a, an, the) author who writes books.
7. Can I please have _____ (a, an, the) Liberian flag?
8. Mr. Foday will come back within _____ (a, an, the) hour.
9. Korto was born into _____ (a, an, the) poor family.
10. Ever been to _____ (a, an, the) waterfall in Kpatawee?
11. I want to talk to one of _____ (a, an the) senators.
12. That big thing is _____ (a, an, the) elephant.
13. I love _____ (a, an, the) Minister of Education.
14. This is _____ (a, an, the) amazing view of the city.
15. Have you ever seen _____ (a, an, the) grasshopper?
16. _____ (a, an, the) Holy Bible is read by most Christians.

# Contractions

## Poem & Contractions: Writing Short Forms Of Words

**A Contraction is a short way of writing two words.**

When writing contractions for words, used an (') apostrophe in the place of the missing letter or letters.

### Examples:

1.) Do + Not = Don't         2.) Can + Not = Can't

Knowing where to put the apostrophe has always been a problem for many students. Don't worry, I will help you learn.

### Here is a little poem about contractions.

#### A Poem About Contractions

To write a contraction is easy

We take some letters out

To put an apostrophe in

We take some letters out

That's the way we must begin

Contractions make writing easy

To write a contraction is as easy as can be!

If you can a write contraction, say yeah.. by E.S. Clarke

# Chapter 5

## Contractions: Writing Short Forms Of Words

**Below is a table containing words and their contractions.**

| | |
|---|---|
| I + am | I'm |
| I + will | I'll |
| You + are | You're |
| He + is | He's |
| It + is | It's |
| She + is | She's |
| We + are | We're |
| Was + not | Wasn't |
| They + are | They're |
| Have + not | Haven't |
| You + have | You've |
| I + have | I've |
| It + will | It'll |
| Did + not | Didn't |
| Is + not | Isn't |
| I + had | I'd |
| Will + not | won't |
| He + will | He'll |
| He + would | He'd |
| Were + not | Weren't |
| Can + not | Can't |
| You + have | You've |
| Does + not | Doesn't |
| Has + not | Hasn't |
| Do + not | Don't |

# Contractions

## CONTRACTIONS: WRITING SHORT FORMS OF WORDS

If you learn how to write contractions, writing and reading will become very easy for you.

**Let us look at these examples with contraction forms.**

1. The motorbikes **don't** move fast like cars.
2. Liberia **isn't** for one person.
3. We **haven't** traveled to Palala before.
4. Liberia **wasn't** really hot like this forty years ago.
5. The President **wouldn't** do anything about his behaviors.
6. That man **can't** see very well.

We can rewrite the above sentences without contractions.

**Examples without contractions**

1. The motorbikes **do not** move fast like cars.
2. Liberia **is not** for one person.
3. We **have not** traveled to Palala before.
4. Liberia **was not** really hot like this forty years ago.
5. The President **would not** do anything about his behaviors.
6. That man **cannot** see very well.

# Chapter 5

**WHAT HAVE WE LEARNED SO FAR? PUTTING IT ALL TOGETHER**

The two Articles are ⟶ Definite and Indefinite article

Definite Article ⟶ describe things we know

Indefinite Articles ⟶ point at a singular noun

'A' is used before a noun ⟶ beginning with a consonant

'An' is used before a noun ⟶ beginning with a vowel

Contractions ⟶ Short form of writing words

**Circle the articles in these sentences below.**

1. The Earth is a planet on which we live.
2. My mother works as a nurse at Harbel Hospital.
3. Jartu's father is an artist.
4. I work for the President of Liberia and not you, my friend!
5. Ms. Herring is an English teacher at my school.
6. Monrovia is the capital city of Liberia.

**Write the Contraction for the words in the sentences below.**

1. David and Flomo <u>did not</u> come to school today. (_____)
2. Ellen <u>does not</u> like to be second in a competition. (_____)
3. Fatima <u>is not</u> in her bed room, mama. (_____)
4. I <u>cannot</u> tell you if Prince and Samuel were here. (_____)
5. Alex and Decontee <u>were not</u> in class Monday. (_____)

# Negative Sentences

## NEGATIVE SENTENCES: CHANGING SENTENCE FORMS

**A Negative Sentence** is a sentence that says something is not correct or true.

### Examples:

1. Jebbeh will cook the food today. (True)

2. Jebbeh will not cook the food today. (Negative)

### Analysis

1.) The first sentence tells us what Jebbeh <u>will</u> do.

2.) The second sentence tells us that Jebbeh <u>**will not**</u> cook.

I am sure, as a first grader, you would be very sad when you hear your mother tells you what Jebbeb will not do.

In short, it is easy to change a true sentence into a negative sentence.

*To change a true sentence into a negative sentence, you use contraction words.*

### Tips:

To change a true sentence into a negative sentence you have to add a negative word to that sentence. **That negative word is '<u>NOT</u>'**

FIGURE 5-15 A picture of a student talking about Negative Sentences

GRADE 1 LANGUAGE ARTS

# Chapter 5

## NEGATIVE SENTENCES: CHANGING SENTENCE FORMS

It can sometimes be fun changing a positive or true sentence to a negative or false sentence.

Before doing such, you need to know the negative words that can change a true sentence into a negative sentence.

**Below is a table containing negative contraction words.**

| Negative words + Contraction | True sentence | Negative |
|---|---|---|
| do + not = don't | We eat rice. | We don't eat rice. |
| does + not = doesn't | She lives here. | She doesn't live here. |
| is + not = isn't | He is coming. | He is not coming. |
| will + not = won't | I will eat rice. | I won't eat rice. |
| have + not = haven't | I have been here. | I haven't been here. |
| did + not = didn't | I did my work. | I didn't do my work. |
| are + not = aren't | You are sleepy. | You are not sleepy. |
| was + not = wasn't | He was in school. | He wasn't in school. |
| has + not = hasn't | She has gone in. | She hasn't gone in. |
| can + not = can't | I can see at night. | I can't see at night. |

**Find the word that will change the true (positive) sentence into a (false) negative sentence.**

1. Marbutu _____ eat pig feet. (has not, didn't, doesn't)
2. Yah and Mamie _____ live here. (do not, haven't, didn't)
3. I _____ be a bad citizen. (don't, will not, hasn't,)
4. Mr. Kanneh _____ given me money. (isn't, hasn't, didn't)
5. The President _____ lived in America. (aren't, hasn't, doesn't)

# Compound Words

## COMPOUND WORDS: JOINING WORDS

**A Compound word** is two small words that are joined together to form a new word.

Compound words are mainly naming words that we often refer to as nouns.

### Examples:

1.) Police + man = policeman    2.) book + bag = bookbag

Every Compound word has two primary parts.

1. The first part tells us about the person or thing.
2. The second part identifies or shows the person or thing in question.

### Analysis

1. Police + man = Policeman: in this word, the first part tells us that the noun is a police. The second part identifies the noun as a man. Therefore we have the word **policeman**.

2. Book + bag = Bookbag: in this word like the other word, the first part tells us that the object or thing is a book. The second part also identifies the object or thing as a bag. Therefore we have the word **bookbag**.

> Compound words help build students' vocabulary.
> corn + meal = cornmeal, sun + shine = sunshine
> rain + fall = rainfall, air + port = airport

GRADE 1 LANGUAGE ARTS

# Chapter 5

## COMPOUND WORDS: JOINING WORDS

Below is a table containing compound words to learn and use.

| | | | | |
|---|---|---|---|---|
| anywhere | classroom | eyebrow | handshake | lifetime |
| anytime | cutlass | eyeball | hairstyle | lipstick |
| airport | cowboy | eyeglass | itself | manpower |
| anybody | copybook | football | input | maybe |
| armchair | cabman | fingernail | inside | nowhere |
| bathroom | daylight | footprint | jackpot | nobody |
| bedroom | daytime | gateway | kickball | outside |
| blackboard | daybreak | grandson | kindergarten | peacekeeper |
| bedspread | drumstick | goalkeeper | keyboard | quicksand |
| blackboard | deadline | haircut | lockout | rainbow |

It is very easy to use compound words in sentences. Let us try.

1. I will go to school when **daylight** comes.
2. Uncle Tom will drive to the **airport**.
3. Amelia and Sieneah are playing **kickball**.
4. The **policeman** protects everyone.
5. You do not make noise in the **classroom**.

**Write the correct compound word in the blank space below.**

1. Karla has a beautiful _____ on her head.
2. We have new armchairs in our _____.
3. Bats do not like _____.
4. A _____ has seven colors.
5. At the football game, the _____ caught the ball.

# Compound Words

## Compound Words: A Poem That Rhymes

### Fine Time

I can tell the exact time
Mama give me a dime
And said it was all mine
To go and have a fine time
We sat between the pines
Rolling twines
So papa can tie barrels
To carry his palm wine
Papa said if my spine grew
As tall as the road sign
By the time I turn nine
I can go run around
I laughed and jumped up and down
Thinking how my friends and I
Could create big big circle lines
And dance and dance around
That is what I call fine fine time!......by Miatta S. Herring

# Chapter 5

**WHAT HAVE WE LEARNED SO FAR? PUTTING IT ALL TOGETHER**

Compound words ➤ two words that are joined

Compound words are ➤ naming words or nouns

Compound words have ➤ two parts

The first part ➤ talks about the noun

The second part ➤ identifies noun in question

A look at compound words. Write the correct word below.

1. Wind + shield = _____

2. My teacher writes our notes on a _____ everyday.

3. The old man is wearing dark _____ over his eyes.

4. School + house = _____

5. I have a new _____ to write my note in.

6. Grand + mother _____

7. _____ bread comes from corn.

8. Eye + glass = _____

9. Arm + chair = _____

10. She does not allow _____ to play with her toys.

11. Mustapha's _____ lives in the Executive Mansion.

# Chapter 5 Review

## LET'S FIND OUT

**Follow the instructions and answer all questions correctly.**

1. There are 4 kinds of vowels in the English language T/F\_\_\_

2. There are 25 consonants in the English Language T/F\_\_\_

3. On a clean sheet, list the vowels in the English Language.

4. _____ show relationship between letters and sounds.

5. What is a consonant blend?

6. Underline the consonant blend in the below words.

    1. bus    2. clap    3. apple    4. blue

    5. grape    6. door    7. flat    8. sun

7. A Verb that tells you what a noun is doing is called _____?

8. Who is Ma Hawa in the story, "Fatu and the Tricky Blind Man?"

9. _____ was the name of the blind man. The man was not blind at all. T/F _____

10. There are two types of articles in English. T/F _____

11. _____ is a special kind or adjective used in English.

12. The two types or articles are _____ and _____.

13. What is a definite article?

# Chapter 5 Review

## LET'S FIND OUT

14. You use the word or article ____ if you know the noun.

15. Underline the <u>definite article</u> once and <u>indefinite article</u> twice.

    1. Sieneah Weawea is shaking the President's hand.

    2. Yagorpu Suah is an excellent friend to be with.

    3. This is an English book.

    4. The capital city of Bong County is Gbarnga.

16. Use the article 'An' before nouns beginning with vowels.

17. The two main indefinite articles are _____ and _____.

18. _____ is a short way of writing two small words into a new word.

19. Write the contracted or regular form for the below words.

    1. cannot = _____   2. has not = _____   3. don't = _____

    4. was not = _____   5. haven't = _____   5. are not = _____

20. A negative sentence says something is not true. T/F __

21. What is a compound word?

22. A compound word has four main parts .T/F _____

23. The _____ part tells us about the person or thing.

**Next Chapter**

# CHAPTER SIX OBJECTIVES

Parts of Speech Review ...131  Interjection ..................133
Noun ..............................131  Singular Noun ..............136
Pronoun .........................131  Singular Noun ..............136
Verb ...............................131  Plural Noun ..................137
Adverb ...........................132  How Lib. Was Founded...140
Adjective ........................132  Dramatization ...............141
Preposition .....................132  Fun With Poems............144
Conjunction ...................132  Writing Corner .............146

# Review of English

## REVIEW OF THE ENGLISH LANGUAGE: HOW ENGLISH BEGAN

**How did English come about and how do we learn it?**

English is a very hard language to learn.

English comes from many different languages in Europe.

English comes from French, Spanish, German, and a native British dialect from the North of Great Britain.

To be able to speak and write English very well, one has to first learn the letters of the English Alphabet.

There are 26 letters in the English Alphabet.

Once the 26 letters of the alphabet are mastered by a student, that student can then learn to create words by putting letters of the alphabet together.

Any kind of word can be formed by combining these letters.

### Examples:

1. Africa  2. Apple  3. Ball  4. Beans  5. Cat  6. Dog  7. Elephant  8. Mosquito  9. Pumpkin  10. Bread  11. Lantern  12. Crab

To master the English Language, you must know how to read and write the Eight Parts of Speech.

The Eight Parts of Speech are eight groups of words that help students write, read, and speak proper English.

# Chapter 6

## REVIEW OF THE EIGHT PARTS OF SPEECH

**The Eight Parts of Speech are as follows:**

1. Noun
2. Pronoun
3. Verb
4. Adverb
5. Adjective
6. Preposition
7. Conjunction
8. Interjection

*A review of the Eight Parts of Speech*

Now let us review the Eight Parts of Speech individually.

I. **A Noun** names a person, a place, a thing or an idea.

### Examples:

1. **John** = a person   2. **Liberia** = a place   3. **rock** = a thing

II. **A Pronoun** is a word that replaces a noun.

### Examples:

1. **Wehtee** is a girl.   2. **She** is my best friend.

III. **A Verb** is an action word. It shows what the noun is doing.

### Example:

1. George Weah will **kick** that football into the goalpost.

**Why is it good to learn the Eight Parts of Speech?**
If you learn the Eight Parts of Speech, you will know how to write and speak better English. Liberia needs you!

# Review Parts of Speech

## REVIEW OF THE EIGHT PARTS OF SPEECH

**IV. An Adverb** is a word that describes a verb or an adjective.

**Examples:**

1. My puppy eats **quickly**.  2. Teah **slowly** walked to the door.

**Tips:**

Most adverbs that describe a verb end in 'ly'. Look above at the previous two sentences, (**quickly** and **slowly**).

**V. An Adjective** is a word that describes a noun or a pronoun.

**Examples:**

1. That girl has **beautiful** brown eyes.  2. The ship is **big**.

**VI. A Preposition** is a word that shows a relationship between nouns and other words in a sentence.

**Examples:**

1. I walked **through** the door.  2. She is **under** the table.

**VII. A Conjunction** is a word that joins two sentences together.

**Examples:**

1. I like Fufu **and** Palm Butter. 2. I like dogs **but** not cats.

**Tips**: The three main Conjunctions are: **and**, **but**, & **when**.

# Chapter 6

## REVIEW OF THE EIGHT PARTS OF SPEECH

**VIII.** An **Interjection** is a word that expresses a strong emotion.

### Examples:

1. WOW! This place is beautiful. 2. Oh my God! This is great!

**Tips**: Most interjections are followed by an exclamation mark.

Examples are: OUCH! OH NO! HEY! WOW! OMG!

FIGURE 6-1 A picture of students standing in line at devotion at an elementary school as they keep conversation using Liberian English, also known as Colloquial. As a student, avoid speaking this form of language in school and in a learning environment. Always try to speak standard English at all times. Whenever your schoolmates or classmates laugh at you and call you Mr./Ms. America, do not let that bother you.

# Review of The Alphabets

## REVIEW OF LETTERS OF THE ALPHABET: AN OVERVIEW

Let us put these pictures in the correct alphabetical order.

_____

_____

_____

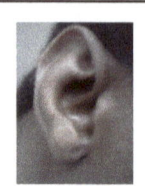
_____

_____

_____

_____

_____

_____

_____

_____

_____

_____

_____

_____

_____

_____

_____

# Chapter 6

## REVIEW OF LETTERS OF THE ALPHABET: AN OVERVIEW

Let us put these pictures in the correct alphabetical order.

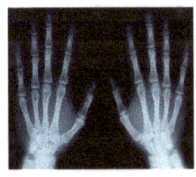      

_____   _____   _____

_____   _____   _____

_____   _____

From the below letters and words, circle all the capital letters.

```
        s   Z    Harbel  f  C  Totota   V  f  e
  Monrovia  Baby g      Paynesville  k  cassava leaves  D  s
s    D    a    M   r    d    q    P    S    z    L    K    X
d V   w  Y  k   A  n   N  m  1  Z  C  b    G   q  P   H
F    Q   w    E   r    T   y    u  i   O   p    a   S   d   6
r  d   F   G  s   h   J  k  l  9   Z  3   t  x   4  V   5
q    7    B   N   r    8    M  I    g    j    10   o   H
  a  Konola,  r  Lonestar  C  y  J  w  4  h  M  k  9  f
     D  Liberia   c s D  v g  lapa   kily wily  ground pea
              R  West Point    MoE   m   e
```

# Review of Singular Nouns

## REVIEW OF SINGULAR NOUNS: A NOUN WITHOUT 'S'

A **Singular noun** talks about only one person, place, thing, or idea.

### Examples:

1. Moses Dekai has one **German Plum** in his pocket.
2. Foday has only one **bookbag** for school.
3. The school principal has a black **car**.
4. Finda and her sister have a **book** on their desk.

### Analysis

In the sentences above, all of the nouns, German Plum, bookbag, car, and book do not have 'S' at the end of the noun.

**Tips**: Singular nouns usually do not have 's' at the end of the word.

Below is a table containing singular nouns.

| hand | cup | farm | pepper | eye |
|---|---|---|---|---|
| mouth | ear | nose | foot | arm |
| egg | hen | mat | rooster | egg |
| rooster | hill | pen | pencil | rat |
| fish | spoon | bowl | pot | tree |

➡ A last quick look at Plural Nouns: the nouns with 'S"

136

# Chapter 6

## REVIEW OF PLURAL NOUNS: A NOUN WITH AN 'S'

A **Plural noun** talks about more than one person, place, thing, or idea.

### Examples:

1. Munah has two **spoons** in her bag.
2. Humans have two **hands** and two feet.
3. There are twelve **months** in the year.
4. There are also seven **days** in the week.

### Analysis

In the sentences above, all of the nouns: spoons, hands, months, and days, all have 'S' at the end of the noun.

**Tips**: Singular nouns do not always have 'S' at the end of the word.

#### Below is a table containing plural nouns.

| hands | cups | farms | peppers | eyes |
|---|---|---|---|---|
| mouths | ears | noses | phones | arms |
| eggs | hens | mats | balls | legs |
| roosters | hills | pens | pencils | rats |
| peaches | spoons | bowls | pots | trees |

Plural nouns almost always have an 's' at the end of the word. Never add an "S" to a person's first name.

GRADE 1 LANGUAGE ARTS

# Review of Rhymes

## RHYMES: A LOOK AT EVERYDAY WORDS

**A Rhyme is when one or two or more words have the same ending sounds**.

If you put special words, numbers, and facts into rhymes, you will easily remember them.

**Example:**

30 days hath September

April, June, and November

All the rest have 31 days

Except for February, it has 28 days

**Some rhymes can be sung. Just try the one above and you will see what I am talking about.**

From the example above, tell your teacher which month has 30 days and which has 31 days. Do not look back at the rhyme!

1. January, August, September and November

2. September, April, June and February

3. November, June, September and April

4. May, August, March and July

5. December, October, January and May

# Chapter 6

## RHYMES: A LOOK AT EVERYDAY WORDS

In the Table below are everyday words that rhyme.

| Salala | Palala |
|--------|--------|
| Kakata | Totota |
| Bendaja | Kendeja |
| pot | hot |
| meat | seat |
| sea | bee |
| bread | dread |
| hat | mat |
| like | bike |
| cut | nut |

**Circle the correct words that rhyme from the below list.**

1. blade        care        glad        trade
2. dust         lost        burst       lust
3. May          Zienzu      Ganta       Klay
4. play         say         friend      day
5. end          bend        mean        trend
6. bill         last        thrill      will
7. skate        make        late        great
8. and          ball        call        tall

GRADE 1 LANGUAGE ARTS

# Story And Dramatization

**STORY AND DRAMATIZATION: STORIES IN OUR OWN WORDS**

### How Liberia Was Founded: A folklore.....by E.S. Clarke

Many years ago, a great God came down from the sky and dried up all the water from the land. Soon trees grew, and animals large and small appeared on all the lands on the Earth.

The God of the sky then put people all over the Earth. In Liberia, he placed very special people. The people in Liberia were not that many. They were mostly on the coast, starting from Grand Cape Mont County all the way to Grand Bassa.

The people in Liberia at that time were very happy and were glad that the God of the sky had put them there. After God had placed them on the land, people from other parts of Africa began to move into Liberia also. This made the people in Liberia very unhappy. Their king was very unhappy too.

Many of the people that were coming to Liberia came because of different reasons. Some of them were running away from wars, while others came from across the ocean because they had been set free after being in slavery for so many years.

Today in Liberia, boys and girls from various backgrounds can play, live and work together. The God of the sky made Liberia for everyone. In our schools, there are boys and girls that belong to different tribes. No matter who you are or what tribe you belong to, we are all Liberians and Liberia belongs to all of us!

## Chapter 6

**STORY AND DRAMATIZATION: STORIES IN OUR OWN WORDS**

### Dramatization

With the help of your teacher, dramatize how Liberia was founded by using the story you just read on the previous page.

### Characters

1. The original people that were living in Liberia
2. The people that came to Liberia from other parts of Africa
3. The people that came to Liberia from across the ocean

### Plot

Let the original people living in Liberia demonstrate how they were living before other people came in their country.

Let the people that came and joined the original Liberians demonstrate how difficult or easy things were for them when they came to live in Liberia.

Discuss among yourselves how you would have behaved when someone escaping wars or having been in slavery for more than 200 years comes to live in your country.

Now that you all are living happily ever after in present day Liberia, would you accept another group of people from another country to come and live in Liberia or within your neighborhood? Why or why not?

# Review of The Year

## How The Year Goes: Making Sense of Things

**Know the days of the week and the months of the year:**

There are 60 minutes in one hour.

There are 24 hours in one day.

There are 7 days in one week.

There are 4 weeks in one month.

There are 12 months in one year.

There are 365 days in the year.

There are 52 weeks in one year.

There are 8,766 hours in one year.

**The names of the 7 days of the week are as follows:**

1. Sunday  2. Monday  3. Tuesday  4. Wednesday
5. Thursday  6. Friday  7. Saturday

**The names of the 12 months of the year are as follows:**

1. January  2. February  3. March
4. April  5. May  6. June
7. July  8. August  9. September
19. October  11. November  12. December

# Chapter 6

## WHAT HAVE WE LEARNED SO FAR? PUTTING IT ALL TOGETHER

1. English comes from ⟶ many languages in Europe
2. The alphabet ⟶ has 26 unique letters
3. Noun names ⟶ a person, a place or a thing
4. Pronoun is a word ⟶ used in place of a noun
5. Verb is ⟶ an action word
6. Adverb ⟶ describes verb or an adjective
7. Adjective ⟶ describes a noun or pronoun
8. Preposition shows ⟶ relationship between nouns
9. Conjunction joins ⟶ two sentences together
10. Interjection ⟶ expresses strong emotion
11. Singular noun is ⟶ about one person or thing
12. Plural noun is ⟶ about more than one person
13. Rhyming words ⟶ have the same sound
14. The Eight Part of Speech are eight unique words T/F ___
15. To learn English you must know the Alphabet T/F ___
16. Liberia was founded by _____ groups of people.
17. The people from across the ocean were free slaves T/F___
18. The other people came because of wars T/F _____

# Fun With Poems

## Fun With Poems: A Poem That Rhymes Is Fun

### A Plan

Our teacher said
Everything you do
Must have a plan
Before it lands
So we all took our pencil

And drew our own airplane
To show how it would look
On the runway at Robertsfield
We made rails using nails
For people to stand

When they got out of their van
In front was a sign
That read 'Beware'
If you have small children
You must hold their hands

Then we added a gate
Just in case the plane came late
We could all sit and wait
But if it did not make it
Everyone will bid each other
Farewell and head Straight to bed
Now that is why plans are important!

..........by Miatta S. Herring

# Chapter 6

## The First Graders' Workshop: Writing Activities

### Write Your Own Poem

Your Name: _____

**Grade 1 Language Arts**

# Writer's Corner

## The First Graders' Workshop: Writing Activities

My name is: _____  Date: _____

In the table below, write what first graders **are**, **have**, and **can**.

### First Graders

| are | have | can |
|-----|------|-----|
|     |      |     |
|     |      |     |
|     |      |     |
|     |      |     |
|     |      |     |
|     |      |     |
|     |      |     |
|     |      |     |

# Chapter 6

## THE FIRST GRADERS' WORKSHOP: WRITING ACTIVITIES

My name is: _____    Date: _____

From the list of words you created on page 146, choose your favorite from the column and circle it. Then neatly write it in the corresponding box below.

*First graders are*

*First graders have*

I love being in the first grade

*First graders can*

This is why I love being in the first grade in Liberia.

GRADE 1 LANGUAGE ARTS

# Writer's Corner

## THE FIRST GRADERS' WORKSHOP: WRITING ACTIVITIES

My name is: _____  Date:_____

**From Chapter 1, neatly write 26 new words that you learned in that chapter in the blank space provided below.**

1. _____ 2. _____ 3. _____ 4. _____

5. _____ 6. _____ 7. _____ 8. _____

9. _____ 10. _____ 11. _____ 12. _____

13. _____ 14. _____ 15. _____ 16. _____

17. _____ 18. _____ 19. _____ 20. _____

21. _____ 22. _____ 23. _____ 23._____

24. _____ 25. _____ 26. _____

Choose any 8 of the words and neatly create a sentence out of each of them. Use proper grammar and the correct end mark.

1. _____

2. _____

3. _____

4. _____

5. _____

6. _____

7. _____

8. _____

# Chapter 6

## The First Graders' Workshop: Writing Activities

Grade 1 Language Arts

# Writer's Corner

## THE FIRST GRADERS' WORKSHOP: WRITING ACTIVITIES

Using the picture on page 149, neatly write about what you saw in that picture.

Use the words in the table to help you with your writing.

1. My mother goes to the _____.
2. She goes there to _____.
3. The ground has _____.
4. Other people go there to _____.
5. To go to the market people take _____.
6. After selling, people do not sweep the _____.
7. To buy things we need _____.
8. The market is always _____.

| sell | food |
|------|------|
| market | buy |
| dirty | steal |
| water | car |
| mud | clothes |
| noisy | shoes |
| money | book |
| price | pencil |
| bike | girl |
| good | |

**Look at that picture and write some things that you see.**

1. _____
2. _____
3. _____
4. _____
5. _____
6. _____
7. _____

# Chapter 6

## THE FIRST GRADERS' WORKSHOP: WRITING ACTIVITIES

**Using Chapter 2, neatly do the following as instructed.**

I. Write 6 of the Golden Rules of Courtesy and Respect.

DO's                              DON'Ts

1. _____          2. _____

3. _____          4. _____

5. _____          6. _____

II. Write a morning dialogue between you and a friend.

**You**                           **Your Friend**

1. _____          2. _____

3. _____          3. _____

4. _____          5. _____

III. Write five naming words and five special naming words.

1. _____ 2. _____ 3. _____ 4. _____ 5. _____

1. _____ 2. _____ 3. _____ 4. _____ 5. _____

IV. Write the Eight Parts of Speech and discuss them in class.

1. _____ 2. _____ 3. _____ 4. _____

5. _____ 6. _____ 7. _____ 8. _____

GRADE 1 LANGUAGE ARTS

# Writer's Corner

## THE FIRST GRADERS' WORKSHOP: WRITING ACTIVITIES

**Using Chapter 3, neatly do the following as instructed.**

I. Write these singular and plural nouns into sentences.

1. cup _____ 2. dog _____

3. pen _____ 4. mat _____

1. tubs _____ 2. caps _____

3. boys _____ 4. girls _____

II. Write these verbs into sentences. Use the correct end mark.

1. angry _____ 2. eat _____

3. run _____ 4. laugh _____

III. Write these verbs-to-be into sentences.

1. I am _____ 2. Your are _____

3. She is _____ 4. He is _____

IV. Use the following preposition in sentences.

1. in _____ 2. under _____

3. over _____ 4. from _____

V. Name and define the four types of sentences.

1. _____ 2. _____ 3. _____ 4. _____

# Chapter 6

## THE FIRST GRADERS' WORKSHOP: WRITING ACTIVITIES

**Using Chapter 4, neatly do the following as instructed.**

I. Write these descriptive adjectives into sentences.

1. tall _____  2. wet _____

3. small _____  4. hot _____

5. dark _____  6. red _____

7. beautiful _____  8. hungry _____

9. shining _____  10. hit _____

II. Write these demonstrative nouns into sentences.

1. this _____  2. that _____

3. these. _____  4. such _____

5. those _____.  6. them _____

III. Write these personal pronouns into sentences.

1. I _____  2. Me _____

3. he _____  4. _____

5. it _____  6. her _____

7. him _____  8. they _____

GRADE 1 LANGUAGE ARTS

# Writer's Corner

## THE FIRST GRADERS' WORKSHOP: WRITING ACTIVITIES

**Using Chapter 5, neatly do the following as instructed.**

I. Write the six types of vowels in the English Language.

1. ___   2. ___   3. ___   4. ___   6. ___

II. Find the first letter or letters for the following words.

1. _ at   2. _ an   3. _ _ ple   4. _ ed   5. _ oat

6. _ nt   7. _ lap   8. _ og   9. _ ad   10. _ _ ank

III. With the initial consonant blend, write the correct word.

1. cl_ _   2. bl_ _k   3. gr_ _   4. fr_ _   5. sp_ _ _

6. pl_ _   7. cl_ _k   8. fl_   9. dr_ _k   10. pr_ _

IV. Create new words from the following consonant blends.

| Word | New Word |
|---|---|
| 1. Block | |
| 2. Glass | |
| 3. Flap | |
| 4. Clog | |

V. Use the following action verbs in sentences.

1. sleep _____   2. run _____

3. dance _____   3. clap _____

VI. Read Fatu and the Blind Man and create your own story.

VI. Put the following indefinite articles into sentences.

1. a _____   2. an _____

3. She lives in ___ house.   4. We heard ___ amazing story.

# Chapter 6

## The First Graders' Workshop: Writing Activities

VIII. Write the contraction form of the following words.

| Word | Contracted Form |
|---|---|
| do + not | |
| are + not | |
| has + not | |
| was + not | |
| will + not | |
| have + not | |
| cannot | |

IX. Change the positive sentences into negative sentences.

| Positive Sentence | Negative Sentence |
|---|---|
| 1. I will go to school today. | |
| 2. I have recess. | |
| 3. Liberia was colonized. | |
| 4. Kakata is in Bong County. | |
| 5. Wante has a fat cat. | |

X. Write the following compound words for the words below.

| Words | Compound Word |
|---|---|
| black + board | |
| cat + fish | |
| police + man | |
| peace + keeper | |
| air + man | |
| class + room | |

# Writer's Corner

## The First Graders' Workshop: Writing Activities

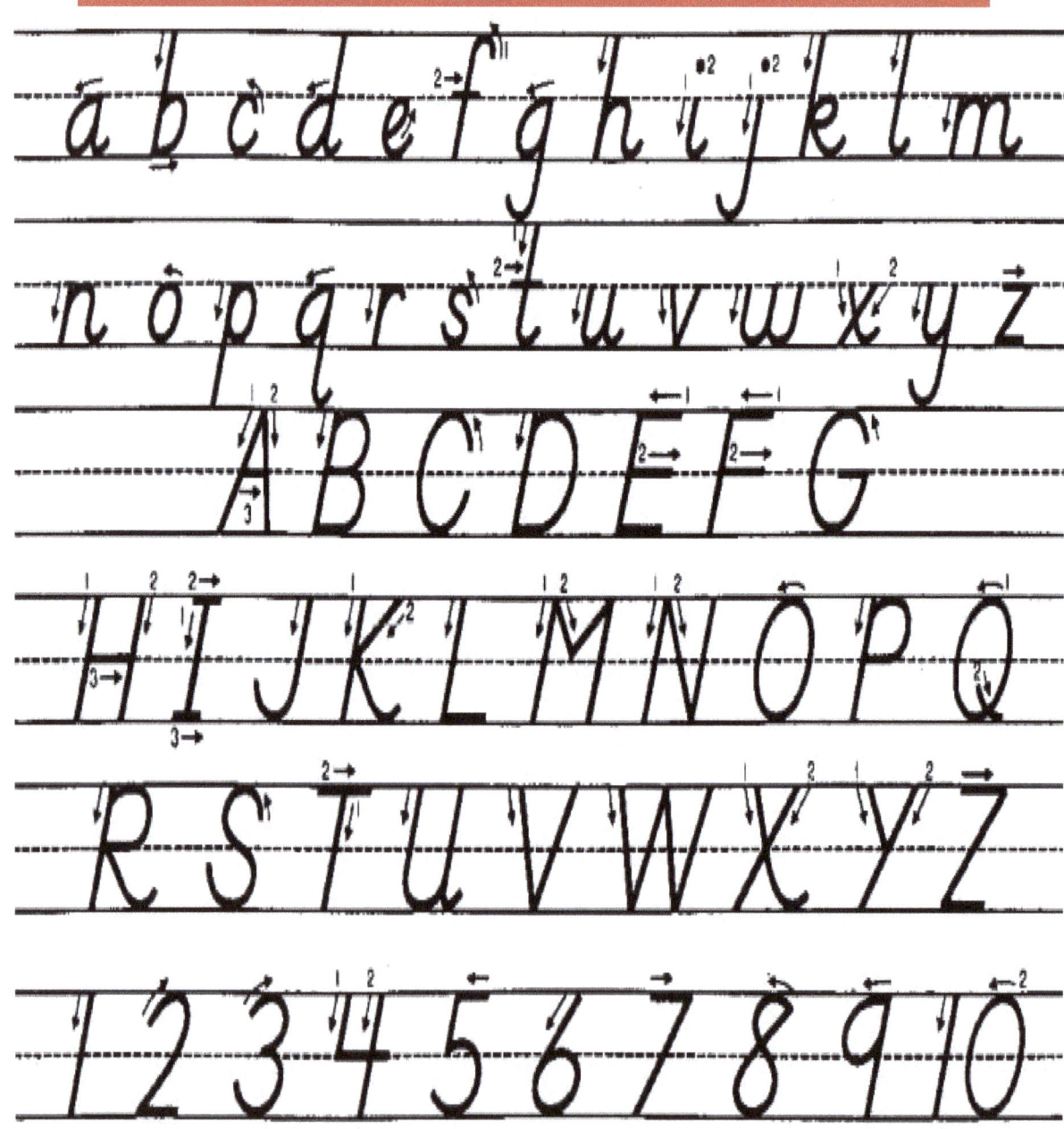

# Chapter 6

## The First Graders' Workshop: Writing Activities

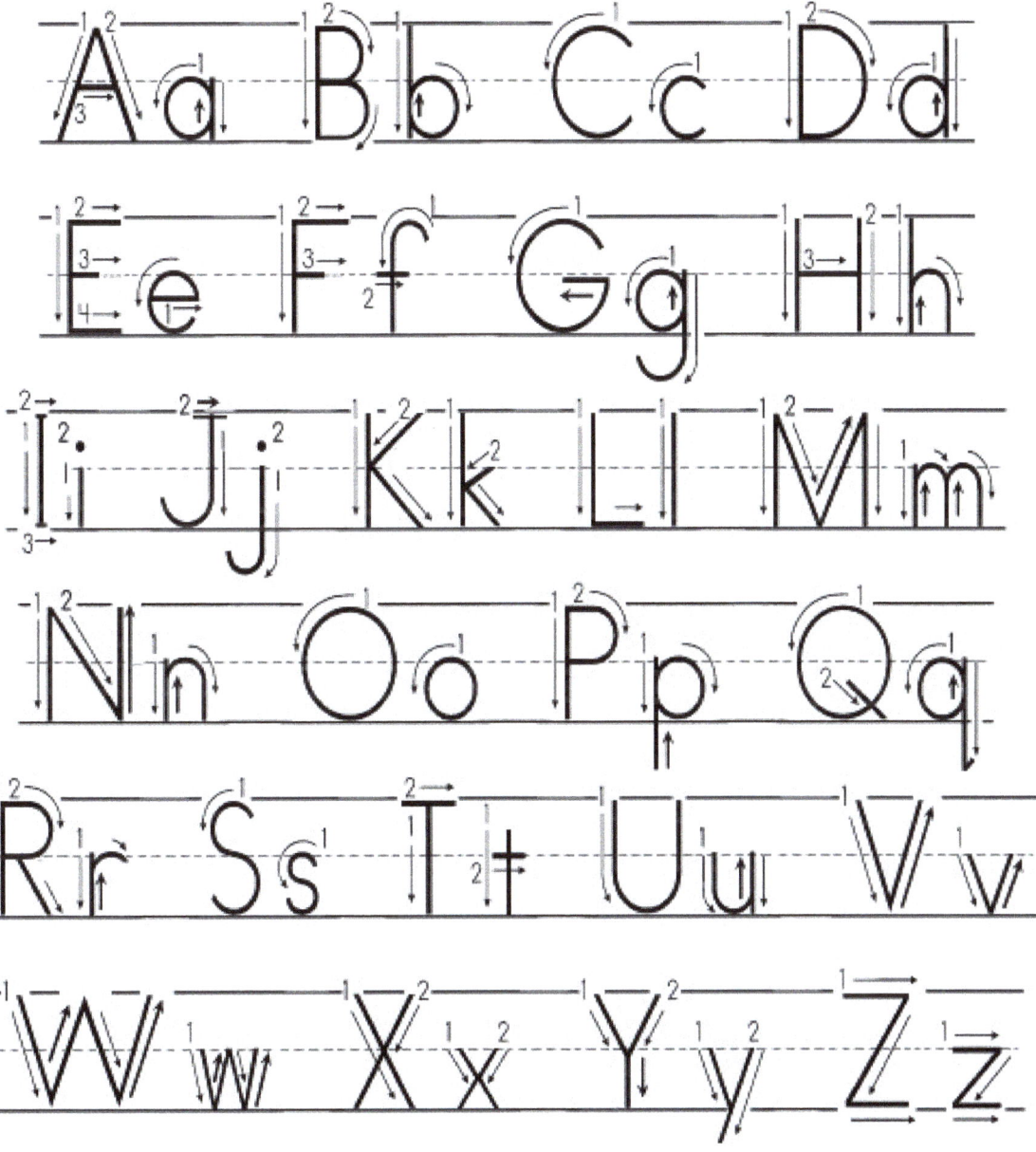

Grade 1 Language Arts

# Writer's Corner

## The First Graders' Workshop: Writing Activities

Aa Bb Cc Dd Ee
Ff Gg Hh Ii Jj
Kk Ll Mm Nn Oo
Pp Qq Rr Ss Tt Uu
Vv Ww Xx Yy Zz

# Chapter 6

## THE FIRST GRADERS' WORKSHOP: WRITING ACTIVITIES

*0 1 2 3 4 5 6 7 8 9*

*zero   one   two   three   four   five*

*six   seven   eight   nine   ten*

*eleven   twelve   thirteen   fourteen   fifteen*

*sixteen   seventeen   eighteen   nineteen   twenty*

GRADE 1 LANGUAGE ARTS

# GLOSSARY

**Africa** Is a continent that has 53 countries. Liberia is located on the Continent of Africa.

**Action Verb** Is a verb that shows action in a sentence.

**Adjective** A word that describes a noun or a pronoun.

**Adverb** Is a word that describes a verb or an adjective.

**Alphabet** 26 unique letters of the English Language that are used to form words.

**Boy** Is a name used to refer to any or all male child.

**Compound Word** Is two small words that are joined together to form a new word.

**Conjunction** Is a word that joins two sentences together.

**Consonant** Five unique letters, A, E, I, O, U from the English Alphabet.

**Consonant Blend** The combination of two or more consonants at the beginning of a word.

**Contraction** A short form of writing two words.

**Courtesy** Is to be polite to others.

**Declarative Sentence** Is a sentence that makes a statement.

**Definite Article** Is a word that points at or describes a thing we know or we have seen before.

**Demonstrative Pronoun** Is a word that identifies or points at a noun.

**Describe** Is to tell how a person or something looks.

# GLOSSARY

## E

**End or Punctuation Mark** It is a mark that brings a sentence to an end or a stop.

**Eight Parts of Speech** Are eight group of words that help students write, read, and speak proper English.

**Exclamation mark** Is an end mark that ends an exclamatory sentence.

**Exclamatory sentence** Is a sentence that expresses a strong feeling or emotion.

## F

**Farmer** A person who makes a farm or a garden.

## H

**Helping verb** is a verb that helps a noun in a sentence.

## I

**Imperative sentence** Is a sentence that gives a command or makes a polite request for something.

**Indefinite pronoun** Is a special kind of adjective that describes or points at a singular noun.

**Interjection** Is a word that expresses a strong emotion.

**Interrogative sentence** Is a sentence that asks a question.

## L

**Linking verb** Is a verb that links a noun to the subject in a sentence.

## N

**Nail** Is a metal or plastic tool used to hold things together.

**Naming word** Are words that name a person, a place, a thing, or an idea.

**Nefertiti** Was a beautiful queen from Egypt.

**Negative sentence** Is a sen-

# GLOSSARY

tence that says something is not correct or true.

**Noun** Is a name of a person, a place, a thing or an idea.

**Orange** Is a fruit that grows on an orange tree.

**Peanut** A seeded plant that grows its seeds underground.

**Period** Is an end mark that ends a declarative sentence.

**Personal pronoun** is a word used in place of a person, people or a thing we are talking about.

**Pet** Any animal kept in the home by people.

**Phonics** Shows the relationship between letters and sounds.

**Plural noun** Any word that talks about more than one person, place, thing, or idea.

**Preposition** Is a word that shows a relationship between nouns and other words in a sentence.

**Pronoun** Is a word used in place of a noun.

**Proper noun** Is the name of a particular person, place, thing or an idea.

**Queen** Is a wife of the king.

**Question mark** Is an end mark that brings a question sentence to an end.

**Rhyme** Is when one of two or more words have the same sounds.

**Respect** Is to show regard for other people or the law.

**Sentence** Is a group of words that make a complete thought.

# GLOSSARY

**Singular noun** Is a noun that names one person, one animal, one place, one thing or one idea.

**The Golden Rules** Are rules and principle needed to guide our behaviors toward one another.

**Title** Is a word the comes before the name of a person.

**Turtle** Is an animal the lives in the wild or in the home as pet.

**Umbrella** Is a circular shaped material used to protect us against rain or the sun.

**Van** A vehicle that is used for transporting people or goods

**Verb** Is a word that shows an action in a sentence.

**Verb-To-Be** Is word that talks about what a person or a group of people are doing most of the time.

**X-Ray** Is a powerful light ray used to see inside the human body.

**Yam** Is a tropical food that grows underground by a yam tree.

**Zoo** Is a park where different animals are kept for people to see.

# INDEX

## A

**A Poem About Singular Noun,** 39, 131

**Action verb,** 106. Also see Verb

**Africa,** 3

**Alphabet,** 3-26

**Adjective,** 72, 112, 132

**Adverb,** 37, 131, 132, 143

## B

**Boy,** 4

## C

**Compound word,** 122-125

**Conjunction,** 37, 131, 132, 143, 156

**Consonant,** 102, 103, 111

**Consonant blend,** 103, 126

**Contraction,** 116-121

**Courtesy,** 30, 31, 41

## D

**Days and week,** 137-138, 142

**Declarative sentence,** 57, 61

**Definite article,** 112

**Describe,** 72

**Dramatization,** 140-141

## E

**Eight Parts of Speech,** 37-39, 46-55

**Exclamation mark,** 60

Exclamatory sentence,

## F

**Farmer,** 3

**Fatu And The Tricky Blind Man,** 107-110

**Fine Time,** 124

## G

**Golden Rules,** 31. See also The Golden Rules

## H

**Helping verb,** 52

**How Liberia Was Founded,** 140

# INDEX

How to treat others, 30

How to Greet Others, 33

How Words Are Created, 8, 14, 19

## I

Imperative sentence, 58

Indefinite article, 112-115, 119

Interjection, 133

Interrogative sentence, 59

## L

L.I.B, 97

Liberians Do Not Answer Questions Directly, 93-95

Linking Verb, 52

## N

Nail, 12

Naming word, 32-36

Nefertiti, 15

Negative word, 120-121

Noun, 34, 38, 131

Number Into Word, 81-88

## O

Orange, 12

Our Journey, 96

## P

Peanut, 15

Period, 60

Personal Pronoun, 79

Pet, 4

Phonics, 102-105

Plural noun, 137

Preposition, 54-55, 131-132

Pronoun, 37, 72-74, 131-132

Proper noun, 35

## Q

Queen, 14

Question mark, 56, 58-59

## R

Rhyme, 89-90

Respect, 30

Rules for Plural, 47

# INDEX

## S

Singular noun, 39-46, 136

## T

The Golden Rules, 31
The Story of Nuumba, 62-66
Title, 36
Turtle, 17

## U

Umbrella, 17

## V

Van, 20
Verb, 48-49 131
Verb-to-be, 49-59

## X

X-ray, 21

## Y

Yam, 21

## Z

Zoo, 22

# PHOTO CREDITS

© Free Stock photo/www.sxc.hu, ©Digital Vision/Getty Images, Google image gallery, Yahoo image gallery, ©Café press, Flikr.com, dailycolorstoday.com, allhatnocattle.net, chrisguillebeau.com, www.fotopedia.com, www.homeroomteacher.com, supernrmal.com, honestlywtf.com, commons.wikimedia.org, www.rubylane.com, www.liberia101.com, latimesblogs.latimes.com, http://mail.colonial.net, http://en.wikipedia.org/wiki/Turtle, thegraphicsfairy.com

## A SPECIAL THANK YOU!

Dear Student:

It was a great pleasure serving you. We look forward to meeting you in the 2nd Grade next year. Please do not forget to access course and other educational materials from our website at: www.clarkepublish.com. Once there, you should click the "Support" link. On the Support page, kindly navigate to *"Grade 1 Language Arts For Liberian Schools: Fundamentals First Edition"* link. There are many interactive activities on our site.

While this might be it for now, we hope to meet you again in the 2nd Grade when you take a journey to explore the English Language. For us at Clarke Publishing and Consulting Group, Inc., we want to be a part of your academic success. This is why we'll be with you every step of the way until you can make it through elementary to junior high school and beyond.

Thank you for choosing us as your English Language Arts partners.


The Clarke Team

www.ingramcontent.com/pod-product-compliance
Lightning Source LLC
Chambersburg PA
CBHW060927170426
43193CB00022B/2980